The Wow's and Why's of Weather

By Mary Kay Carson

S C H O L A S T I C
PROFESSIONAL BOOKS

NEW YORK • TORONTO • LONDON • AUCKLAND • SYDNEY
MEXICO CITY • NEW DELHI • HONG KONG

Dedication

For Tom, who always has an eye on the weather.

Acknowledgments

Many thanks to Deborah Schecter and Tracey West,
fabulous editors with infinite patience.

....

Scholastic Inc. grants teachers permission to
photocopy the student activity pages in this book
for classroom use. No other part of this publication
can be reproduced in whole or in part, or stored in
a retrieval system, or transmitted in any form or by
any means, electronic, mechanical, photocopying,
recording, or otherwise, without written permission
of the publisher. For information regarding permission,
write to Scholastic Inc., 555 Broadway, New York, NY 10012.

....

Cover design by Norma Ortiz

Cover Photos: Thunderstorm: © Richard Kaylin/Tony Stone Images;
Tornado: © Alan R. Moller/Tony Stone Images; Hurricane: © Ernest
Braun/Tony Stone Images; Snowstorm: © Ron Kuntz/Corbis
Interior design by Imagination Ink
Interior illustration by Doug Horne
Science Consultant: Keith Seitter, American Meteorological Society

....

ISBN 0-590-36508-8

Contents

☀ = activity with a reproducible

Introduction

Science is about exploration and discovery. It's a tool for investigating the world around us. There's no better earth science topic to promote the concept of "science as inquiry" to your students than weather. Weather is observable, measurable, and right outside your door. But while weather is an easily accessible science topic, the mechanisms that drive weather systems are complex and many aren't completely understood by today's scientists. Not all of the questions have answers yet—there's still more to learn! Weather provides a wonderful opportunity to challenge students to think for themselves and formulate ideas about how tornadoes form and what brings an "El Niño" year.

About This Book

Take a quick look at the table of contents on page 3. You'll notice that this book is divided into five chapters. The chapters and activities in this book do not need to be used in any particular order. In fact, they are interrelated. After all, it's the sun (Chapter 2) that drives wind (Chapter 4), and what would a hurricane (Chapter 1) be without rain (Chapter 3) to forecast (Chapter 5)? Feel free to integrate the information and activities into your weather unit to best serve your students' needs. Each chapter includes:

Information

Background Information: These pages briefly cover the chapter's topic and its need-to-know facts and scientific principles.

Storm Science: Each chapter includes the science behind a kind of storm connected to the chapter's theme.

Weather and the Environment: Many of today's environmental problems are linked to atmospheric and weather phenomena. Each chapter features an environmental problem that's linked to the chapter's topic.

Cool Weather Career: Each chapter profiles someone working in an interesting weather-related career.

Activities

The activities section includes hands-on investigations for your students. The science topic emphasized in each activity is noted in parentheses after its title in the table of contents.

Build a Weather Station: Each chapter contains background information about a featured weather instrument and instructions for making that instrument in your classroom.

Topic-Related Activities: Activities related to storm science and environmental topics are also included in each chapter.

Extension Activities: Many activities conclude with an activity to expand your students' learning.

Reproducibles: Pages to reproduce and hand out to students follow each chapter's activity section.

Book Breaks: Look for fun ways to use popular fiction and nonfiction books with this weather unit.

Online Links: Find out how to use the web and e-mail to learn more and do more with the weather topics and activities in this book.

Additional Resources

More books for classroom and teacher use, independent reading, related student fiction, and web sites are listed at the end of this book.

National Science Education Content Standards

The information and accompanying hands-on experiments and lessons featured in this book meet many of the National Science Education Content Standards, the set of criteria intended to guide the quality of science teaching and learning in this country. The standards outline key science content areas and support a hands-on, inquiry-based approach to learning. The chart below shows how weather-related topics in this book correlate with the National Science Education Content Standards for both elementary age groups. (Many of these science topics are in parentheses after the activity titles in the table of contents.)

National Science Education Content Standards

Grades K-4*	Grades 5-8
The sun provides the light and heat necessary to maintain the temperature of the earth.	Water evaporates from the earth's surface, cools and condenses into clouds as it rises, and falls as precipitation. This circulation of water between the atmosphere, land, and the oceans and lakes is called the water cycle.
Objects in the sky—such as the sun—have patterns of movement that change their path over the seasons.	The atmosphere consists of a mixture of nitrogen, oxygen, and trace gases including water vapor.
Weather changes from day to day and throughout the seasons.	The atmosphere has different characteristics at different elevations.
Weather can be measured in quantities such as temperature, wind speed and direction, and precipitation.	Clouds affect weather and climate.
* Note that the Science Standards emphasize observing, measuring, identifying, and communicating weather patterns and elements for students in this age group. Understanding the intricacies of the underlying causes of weather—such as air pressure and worldwide currents—is more appropriate study for older students.	Global patterns of atmospheric movement influence local weather.
	The sun's energy drives winds and the water cycle.
	Seasons are a result of the tilt of the earth varying the amount of the sun's energy that reaches the surface of the earth.

Getting Started and Taking It Further

Here are a few ideas for launching—and extending—your class's unit on weather.

Invite students to help guide your weather investigations. Start the unit with a brainstorming session about weather, to find out what most interests your students. Making a KWL chart (What We Know, What We Want to Know, and What We Learned) is a great way to organize those thoughts and to chart progress.

Consider setting up a weather learning center in a corner of your classroom for the duration of the unit. It can incorporate a weather library full of resource books and weather-related story books. The space will not only whet students' appetites for weather, it will provide a focused place for them to go and do independent investigations.

Set up a classroom weather station (or integrate it into the learning center) for measuring weather elements. You can use the instruments made throughout this book, professional instruments, or a combination of both. Have student groups take turns using the instruments to record and report daily the weather for the class. Challenge students to chart the weather conditions over weeks or months and compare.

Designate a section of bulletin board or wall (or again, integrate it into the learning center) for displaying daily weather information such as a weather map from the day's paper or the predicted temperature or wind direction. Students can take turns providing this information from home.

Invite students to keep a Weather Words notebook in which they add words and terms they learn as the unit progresses. Weather journals help students build confidence about what they've learned and can also help with assessment.

Challenge students to develop the activities and investigations in this book into science fair ideas. Many of the suggested extensions make especially good science projects.

Weather Instruments for Your Weather Center:

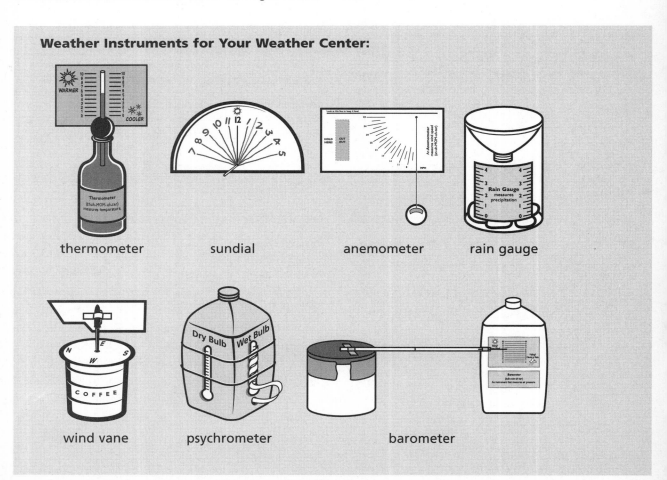

thermometer · sundial · anemometer · rain gauge

wind vane · psychrometer · barometer

The Air Around Us

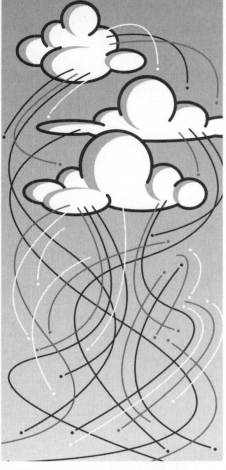

Air's Gases

Nitrogen
76.4%

Oxygen
20.6%

Water
Vapor
2%

Carbon dioxide,
Argon and other
gases. Less than 1%

What Is Weather?

Weather is the condition of the air in a particular place at a specific time. The heat, air pressure, and moisture in the air—or atmosphere—mix and churn to make the weather sunny, cloudy, windy, stormy, or clear.

Weather is not the same thing as climate, however. Climate is a region's regular pattern of weather over a long period of time. The climate in Hawaii may be tropical, but today's weather in Honolulu might be cool and dry. While weather often changes from day to day, a region's climate changes little over the centuries.

The Weight of Air

The atmosphere is the blanket of air that surrounds the earth. It's made up of gases—mostly nitrogen and oxygen with small amounts of water vapor, carbon dioxide, and a few other trace gases. The earth's gravitational pull anchors the atmosphere to the planet and keeps it from drifting off into outer space. Scientists divide the atmosphere into four main layers (see diagram). Air may seem like nothing, but all those molecules of gas have weight and take up space. The weight of the air pushes on the earth's surface, just like a stack of blankets on a table. This pushing force, or air pressure, is about 14.7 pounds per square inch (1 kg/cm²) at sea level. Air pressure lessens with height, however, halving about every 3.4 miles (5.5 km), so there's less air pressure on top of a mountain than at sea level. We're literally living at the bottom of an ocean of air. Air pressure varies not only with height, but also with temperature. Warm air weighs less than cool air, so it rises. (Warm air rises because its fast-moving molecules

Layers of the Atmosphere

Pressure mb (Pa)	Height mi (km)	Approx. Temp. of Layers °F (°C)	Layers of the Atmosphere
	36,000 (60,000)		
	3600 (6000)		
	360 (600)	2200(1200)	thermosphere
10^{-8} (10^{-6})	180 (300)		
0.01 (10)	53 (85)	-150(-100)	
			mesophere
			Ozone Layer
			stratosphere
250 (25,000)	7 (11)	-60(-50)	troposphere
1000	0	68(20)	
100,000			

The layer closest to the ground is the troposphere. It has the most air and moisture of all the layers. It's where the most weather happens.

At the top of the stratosphere—and into the mesosphere—is the ozone layer, the band of O^3, or ozone, that blocks much of the sun's dangerous ultraviolet radiation by absorbing it.

The temperatures in the mesosphere begin to decrease with height, reaching as low as -90°F (-68°C). No commercial aircraft fly this high.

The thermosphere extends from 50 miles (80 km) to 180 miles (288 km) or more. The lower part of the thermosphere is also called the ionosphere and contains electrically charged particles or ions. Radio waves are reflected back to the earth by this layer. Above the thermosphere is interplanetary space, or the exosphere.

Fast Fact

The air around and above us—the atmosphere—weighs 11,000,000,000,000,000,000 lbs (4,950,000,000,000,000,000 kg).

---

spread out, making a volume of warm air less dense or lighter than an equal volume of cool air.)

An area of air that has a higher pressure than its surroundings is called a high-pressure center or system, or simply a high. The sinking air of a high-pressure center dampens the upward movement of air needed for clouds and precipitation to develop. This is why fair weather often accompanies an area of high pressure. In contrast, an area or system of low pressure (or low) has rising air, which encourages cloud and precipitation development. Cloudy weather and likely precipitation are often associated with an area of low pressure. The formation and movement of high- and low-pressure areas in the atmosphere drive much of the weather around the globe.

Low Pressure System

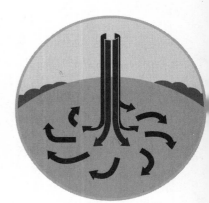

High Pressure System

Storm Science: HURRICANES

Hurricanes are the planet's largest storms. Hurricanes and typhoons—their Pacific Ocean cousins—are typically 300 miles (480 km) in diameter and can have wind gusts in the 150-200 mph (240-320 km per hour) range. They start in the band of warm ocean near the equator when the water is at its warmest. (Hurricane season is June through November for North America and the Caribbean.) Warm water of 80°F (27°C) or more is the required fuel for these giant storms. The moisture from the warm water evaporates into the air hanging above it, creating warm, moist, low-pressure air that's on the rise. As it rises, the air cools and the moisture condenses—releasing tremendous amounts of heat. This released heat warms up the surrounding air, causing it to rise faster and create lower pressure at the surface. Outlying higher pressure air rushes into the new low-pressure area as fast-moving updrafts and eventually a huge whirling mass of air called a tropical depression can form. If the depression continues to be fueled by the heat and low pressure of warm water, it's classified as a hurricane once its winds have reached 74 mph (119 km per hour).

A hurricane's strength is determined by just how low its pressure is. The lower the pressure, the faster and stronger outside air rushes in toward it, so the faster the winds. The low pressure also causes the sea level below the storm to rise, which becomes a flooding mound of water—called a storm surge—if the hurricane hits land. Flooding from storm surges and torrential rains, as in 1998's Hurricane Mitch, causes more hurricane deaths than winds. Hurricanes are rated on the Saffir-Simpson scale of 1 to 5 (next page) which clearly shows how these storms strengthen as their pressure drops.

Category/Damage	1-Minimal	2-Moderate	3-Extensive	4-Extreme	5-Catastrophic
Barometric pressure in inches (of mercury)	more than 28.94	28.50-28.91	27.91-28.47	27.17-27.88	less than 27.17
Wind speed in miles per hour	74-95	96-110	111-130	131-155	more than 155
Storm surge in feet	4-5	6-8	9-12	13-18	more than 18

Weather and the Environment

OZONE LAYER DEPLETION

About 12 to 30 miles (19-48 km) above the earth, near the top of the stratosphere, is the ozone layer, a band of ozone (O_3) gas. The strong sunlight at this altitude acts on molecules of regular oxygen to combine them into ozone and then to subsequently break them down again into oxygen. During this continual recombining process, ozone absorbs some of the sun's ultraviolet (UV) light, shielding the earth from the full force of its harmful effects. Too much UV light can cause skin cancer, cataracts, and can damage plants and plankton.

In the late 1970s, scientists began to notice a thinning of the ozone layer over Antarctica during its spring. This soon-named "hole" in the ozone layer was carefully studied and researchers soon realized that in fact ozone was thinning over both poles. The cause was chlorofluorocarbons (CFCs), super-stable chlorine-containing compounds used in refrigerants like Freon, cleaning solvents for electronics, aerosol propellants, and foam production. After being released, these compounds rise all the way to the stratosphere without breaking down. Once there, the powerful sunlight breaks them down and releases the chlorine which reacts with ozone and destroys it. One CFC molecule can destroy up to 100,000 molecules of ozone. The natural recombining process can't keep up with the chlorine-caused losses, and the ozone layer thins.

The U.S., Canada, Norway, and Sweden banned the use of most CFC-based aerosol propellants in 1979. And the Montréal Protocol treaty of 1987 was signed by 36 nations. It called for a phase-out of all CFC production by the year 2000. Though scientists believe the ozone layer can repair itself given enough chlorine-free time, the CFCs already in the stratosphere will continue eating away at the ozone layer well into the 21st century.

Fast Fact

The energy output of a single hurricane is equivalent to the amount of electricity used in the United States during six months!

Fast Fact

For several days during the winter of 1995-1996, the ozone layer from Greenland to Siberia was depleted by 45%, according to the World Meteorological Organization.

Hurricane Hunter

VALERIE SCHMID

[ONLINE LINK]

Hurricane Hunters Homepage
http//www.
hurricanehunters.com

Join the crew as they take a cyber flight into the eye of a hurricane!

Valerie Schmid is a meteorologist with a dangerous mission. She's a member of the United States Air Force Reserve's 53rd Weather Reconnaissance Squadron — the Hurricane Hunters. These pilots and scientists fly airplanes into the biggest storms on the planet to collect weather data needed to track hurricanes and issue life-saving alerts.

Working inside a plane that's being tossed in high winds and struck by lightning can feel like you're riding "a bucking bronco," Schmid says. But she takes it in stride. "Normally you're just so busy that you're not thinking [that] this might be dangerous," says Schmid. She keeps her eye on the plane's weather instruments that record wind speeds, humidity, temperature, and all-important hurricane-strength air pressure.

Schmid first learned about the Hurricane Hunters from a movie she saw in high school. "I thought, *Wow, what a cool job*. But I never thought I would be able to get a job like that." But after studying meteorology in college and training in weather forecasting after joining the U.S. Air Force, she began to think about flying through hurricanes. "I didn't like the math very much, but I stuck it out because I love science. Those two go hand in hand." After Schmid became a qualified meteorologist in the Air Force, she applied for a Hurricane Hunter position. The competition was tough, but she got the job.

So what's her advice for future Hurricane Hunters out there? "If you have a dream," she says, "go for it!"

Photo courtesy of Valerie Schmid

Key concepts in understanding air pressure and how it influences our weather are knowing that air has weight (mass x gravity), takes up space (volume), and exerts a force (pressure). The three activities that follow will allow your students to discover these properties of air for themselves.

ACTIVITY

Air Is Everywhere

PROPERTIES OF AIR

Air is a combination of invisible gases, so its existence can be difficult for students to comprehend. Challenge students to discover that air has volume in this activity.

Directions

1 Divide the class into small groups. Have students set the funnel inside the neck of the bottle. Ask: *What's in the bottle right now?* (air)

2 Ask students to fill the bottle halfway by pouring water through the funnel. Ask: *Is there air in the bottle now?* (no) *Why not?* (It was displaced by the water.) *How do you think the air got out of the bottle?* (Answers may vary.)

3 Tell students to empty the bottle and replace the funnel. Ask: *What's inside the bottle now?* (air)

4 Have students wrap a "collar" of modeling clay around the mouth of the bottle, sealing it to the funnel. It needs to be airtight!

5 Tell students to try to fill the bottle by pouring water through the funnel. Ask: *What happens?* (The water fills the funnel, but doesn't flow into the bottle.) *Why?* (The air inside the bottle has no way to escape, so the water can't replace it.)

6 Have students poke holes in the clay using the sharpened pencil. Ask: *What happens?* (The water in the funnel drains into the bottle.) *Why?* (The air in the bottle escapes through the holes.)

Extension

Punch one hole in a can of juice. Try pouring liquid out of the can. Punch a second hole in the can and try again. Ask: *How is this similar to the activity we just did?* (With only one hole, the liquid inside the can is held in by trapped air. Punching a second hole allows air to escape and the liquid to pour.)

Materials

(for each group)

water

very narrow funnel

small clear glass bottle (such as a salad dressing bottle)

sharpened pencil

modeling clay

Balancing Balloons

Air has volume and mass. The air inside your classroom alone probably weighs as much as two or three students. This activity will allow students to discover that the invisible gases that make up air have weight, or mass.

Materials

(for each pair of students)

two identical balloons

four 4-inch strips of tape

2- to 3-foot-long thin dowel or yardstick

straight pin

string

Directions

Divide the class into pairs and provide each pair with the above materials. Then have students follow these instructions:

1. Blow up your balloons to equal size, tie them closed, and tape them onto the ends of the dowel using two strips of tape on each balloon.

2. Tie the string near the center of the dowel. One student should hold the string away from his or her partner while the other slides the dowel back and forth until the balloons balance. Ask: *Which balloon is heavier?* (They are equal.)

3. Put a small piece of tape on one of the balloons. While the student holding the string stands still, the other student carefully punctures one of the balloons with the straight pin by sticking it through a taped area. (This will keep the balloon from exploding; the air will seep slowly out instead.)

4. Ask: *What happened?* (The air escaped from the popped balloon, and the full balloon dropped.) *Which side is heavier?* (the full balloon) *Why?* (The air inside the balloon has weight.)

5. Tape and puncture the other balloon and see if the two sides balance.

Pressure vs. Pencil

PROPERTIES OF AIR

Anything that has weight and takes up space exerts pressure, including air. Living under miles of atmosphere is like being under an ocean of air. Water is heavier than air, so a mile of ocean has much more pressure than a mile of air, but the concept is the same. In this activity students can see how air exerts pressure on everything underneath it.

Materials
(for each student)

unsharpened pencil

3 identical sheets of paper

Directions

Provide each student with a set of materials, and have them follow these instructions:

1 Fold one sheet of paper in half and one into quarters. Leave the third sheet as is. Ask: *Which of these papers weighs more?* (None, they are all of equal weight.)

2 Lay the pencil on the end of a desk or table so about two inches of it hangs over the edge. Set the quartered sheet of paper on top of the part of the pencil that is on the desk.

3 Tap the end of the pencil with a quick, but gentle, downward stroke. Ask: *What happens?* (The pencil and paper are knocked to the floor.) *Did you feel a lot of pressure pushing against the paper?* (no) *Was it hard to flip the folded paper?* (no)

4 Repeat steps 2-3 with the halved paper. Make sure to tap the pencil with the same strength you used before. Ask: *What happens? Does it feel harder to flip?* (yes)

5 Repeat steps 2-3 with the open sheet of paper, again using equal force when tapping the pencil. Ask: *What happens?* (The paper doesn't flip.) *How does it feel?* (It feels like there is a lot of pressure pushing down on the paper.) *What is keeping the paper "glued" to the desk?* (The force exerted by the weight of the air over the surface of the paper—air pressure.)

6 Invite students to try all three papers again, comparing the results. Ask: *Why does air pressure hold down the unfolded sheet of paper, but not the others?* (Because it has a larger surface area, more total air pressure pushes down on it.)

Extension

Make a wall chart showing the four layers of the atmosphere. Use a ruler and a marker to divide a piece of butcher paper into four sections based on the proportions of the layers. (See the information box on page 8 for guidance. A scale of 1 cm = 1 km needs about 3 meters in wall height.) Write the name of each layer in each section. Divide the class into four groups and assign each an atmospheric layer. Challenge each group to find out the characteristics of their atmospheric layer, write an informational caption about it, and paste it to the wall chart. Students can include the temperature, gases, atmospheric phenomena, and what kinds of human-made craft travel in their layer. Invite students to illustrate their layer with jets, space shuttles, meteorites, satellites, etc.

Build a Weather Station

MAKE A BAROMETER

S tudents can measure and monitor changes in atmospheric pressure with this easy-to-make barometer. It's fashioned after an aneroid barometer. Note that the units on the scale are not in any standard unit of air pressure. However, students can still use the scale to determine if pressure goes up or down.

Instrument of Interest: **The Barometer**

Air pressure is measured with an instrument called a barometer. A mercury barometer measures mercury as it rises and falls inside a tube, depending on how much air pressure is pushing down on the container in which the mercury sits. An aneroid barometer uses a flexible metal bellows to measure air pressure. The tiny accordion-like sealed cylinder shrinks and expands with changing air pressure. An attached pointer or pen indicates the amount of change on an attached scale.

Directions

1 Cut the neck off of a large balloon. Stretch the balloon top tightly over the can or jar. Use duct tape to secure it to the can or jar and create an airtight seal.

2 Attach two drinking straws together by pinching one and inserting it into the end of the other. They should overlap at least an inch. Tape the toothpick to one end of the combined straws so it sticks out a half-inch or so from the end of the straws. This will be the barometer's indicator needle.

3 Cut out the chart, label, and scale on page 17. Tape the label around the can or jar. Set the scale and chart aside.

4 Lay the non-toothpick end of the combined straws on top of the balloon-covered can or jar. The end of the straws should be in the center of the balloon-covered top. Use a single strip of clear tape to tape the straw onto the top.

5 Set the carton or jug behind the toothpick end of the straw. Tape the scale onto one side of the carton or jug (as shown).

6 Set the barometer indoors in a still area where the temperature doesn't change. Don't set it in a window or other sunny

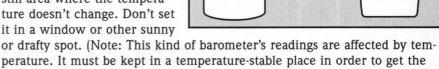

or drafty spot. (Note: This kind of barometer's readings are affected by temperature. It must be kept in a temperature-stable place in order to get the most accurate readings.)

7 Let the barometer settle for a number of hours before taking a first reading. Students can use the chart on page 18 to record the air pressure over time. The toothpick will rise and fall as changes in air pressure contract and expand the balloon, moving the straw.

Mercury Barometer

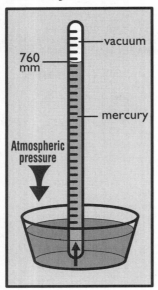

Materials

(for the whole class)

empty coffee can or wide-mouthed jar

large balloon

duct tape

toothpick

clear tape

two drinking straws

reproducible pages 17 and 18

scissors

empty half-gallon jug or carton

Storm Science: Hurricanes

TRACKING DOWN ANDREW

In 1992, Hurricane Andrew plowed through the Bahamas, Florida, and Louisiana, leaving 54 people dead, thousands homeless, and doing $25 billion in damage. It was the costliest hurricane in United States history and the third most intense of the century, with a pressure reading of 27.23 inches when it hit land. Andrew was a powerful category 4 hurricane (see page 9). However, many lives were saved thanks to ample warning and good evacuation plans based on accurate hurricane tracking—the careful following and plotting of a storm's path and development in order to forecast its next step. In this activity students will use actual data to plot the path it took and determine when and where Andrew became a full-blown hurricane.

Materials

for each student)

reproducible pages 19 and 20

ruler

pen, pencil, and crayons, colored pencils, or highlighter pens

tape

Directions

1 Photocopy pages 19 and 20 and distribute to students.

2 Orient students to the map on page 20, reviewing longitude and latitude. Explain that latitude lines are horizontal lines on a globe that measure distance north and south of the equator. Longitude lines are vertical lines on a globe that measure the distance east and west of an imaginary line that passes through Greenwich, England. (Note: If these terms are too advanced for students, simply refer to "degrees North" and "degrees West.")

3 Read through Storm Update 1 as a class. Review the terms, and together locate the first point on the map, which has already been marked. (Note: All positions have been rounded to the nearest whole degree and all wind speeds to the nearest mile per hour. Times are Eastern Standard Time.)

4 Allow students on their own or in pairs to finish plotting the remaining 11 points according to the instructions on page 19. Encourage them to mark their predictions in pencil before plotting the next position.

5 After students have finished plotting the points and connecting them, ask them to color the track based on the storm's wind speed.

Answer

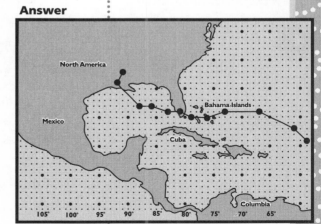

Extension

Challenge student groups to come up with an evacuation schedule for Hurricane Andrew. When should each area be told to evacuate? Note that it takes about 12 hours to evacuate an area.

ACTIVITY

Screening Out the Sun

Weather and the Environment: OZONE LAYER DEPLETION

Materials
(for each group)

four tuna, cat food, or other similarly sized cans with top and bottom removed

sheet of colored construction paper

three different 4-inch square filters (clear plastic wrap, colored plastic wrap, waxed paper, newspaper, cloth, aluminum foil, glass, etc.)

tape

No Filter	Foil
Gauze	Wax Paper

The layer of upper atmospheric ozone gas screens out a good deal of harmful ultraviolet light, preventing it from reaching the earth's surface. In this activity, students will have the opportunity to test the sun-blocking effects of a number of filters.

Directions

Divide the class into small groups and provide each group with one set of the materials listed. Then have students follow these instructions:

1 Assemble the filters by taping each filter onto the end of a can. Leave one can uncovered.

2 Divide the construction paper into quarters and label one square NO FILTER and the other three with the kind of filters you chose. Predict which filter will block out the most sunlight and which will block out the least. Write down your predictions.

3 Put the cans with filters on top of the corresponding squares marked on the page and carefully tape them in place. Set the sheet of construction paper and filters in a sunny windowsill. (Using a stiff notebook or book as a tray will help get it there.)

4 Leave the filters in the sun for a week. Then remove the filters and compare the results. Ask: *What materials blocked the most sunlight? the least? How close were you to your predictions?* (Answers will vary.) *What happened to the paper with no filter?* (The sun bleached out some of the dye.) *How are the filters like the ozone layer?* (They block out some of the sun's rays.)

Book Break

Air Alert: Rescuing the Earth's Atmosphere by Christina G. Millert and Louise A. Berry (Contributor) (Atheneum, 1996). After students read about the causes of atmospheric problems and some solutions, challenge them to make an informational bulletin board showing the kinds of products and sources of renewable energy that do not pollute the atmosphere.

Make a Barometer

Photocopy and cut out one label and one scale for each barometer you make.

Barometer

(buh-rom-eh-ter)

An instrument that measures air pressure.

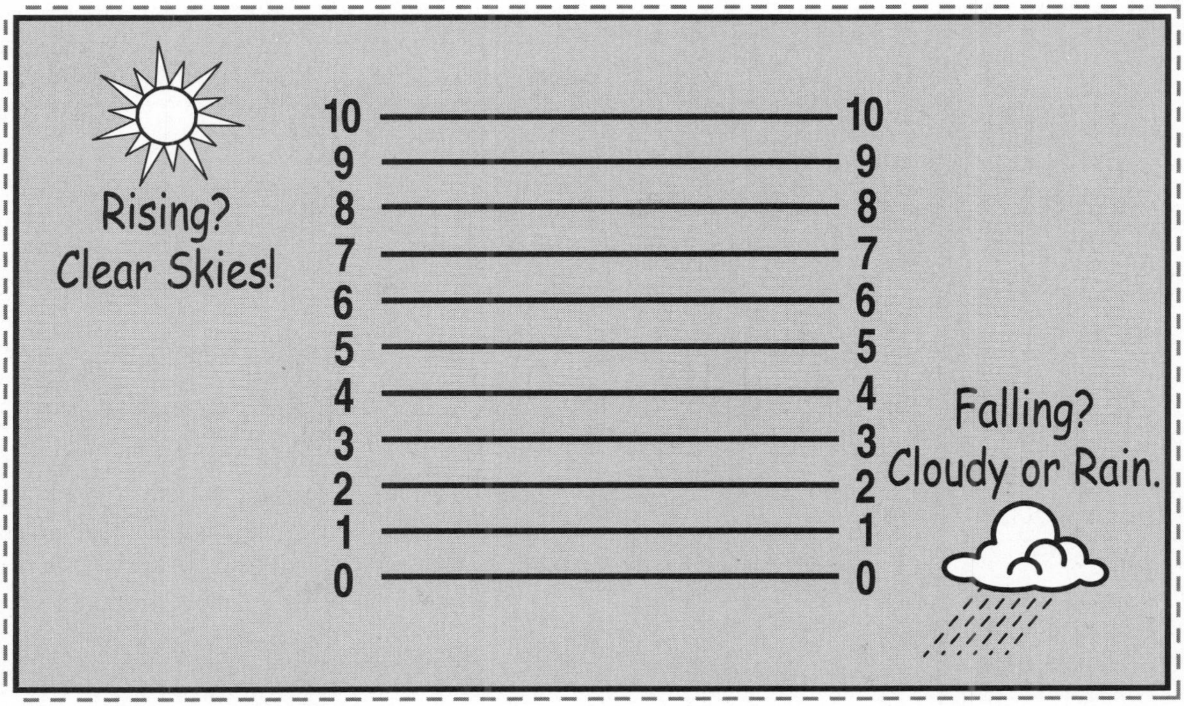

Rising?
Clear Skies!

10	———————	10
9	———————	9
8	———————	8
7	———————	7
6	———————	6
5	———————	5
4	———————	4
3	———————	3
2	———————	2
1	———————	1
0	———————	0

Falling?
Cloudy or Rain.

The Wow's and Why's of Weather Scholastic Professional Books

Name _____

Barometer Watch

Read the barometer every day for two weeks and fill in the chart.

Do you notice any changes in the weather when the barometer reading goes up or down?

Date	Time	Reading	Sunny, Cloudy, or Rainy?

The Wow's and Why's of Weather Scholastic Professional Books

Name _____

Plot Andrew's Path

Hurricane Andrew tore through Florida in August 1992. The powerful hurricane killed 54 people and injured more, but many lives were saved thanks to hurricane-tracking scientists. They carefully follow a hurricane's path and try to predict where it will go next. Then they can warn people ahead of time. Use the Storm Updates to track Andrew's path on your own. Here's how:

1 Look at the 12 Storm Updates below. Notice how each gives a date, a time, a north and west position, and a wind speed. The first Storm Update is already marked on the map.

2 Plot the position for Storm Update 2 on the map. Using a ruler, connect the two points in pen.

3 Now try to guess where the storm will go next. Draw a short line in pencil from the Storm Update 2 position to where you think it will go.

4 Plot the position for Storm Update 3. Use a ruler and a pen to connect it to the last point. How close was your guess?

5 Repeat steps 3 and 4 until all 12 positions are plotted and connected in pen. How does your pencil trail compare?

Storm Updates

1	2	3	4
20 August, 7 A.M. Wind: 46 mph North: 22° West: 61°	21 August, 1 A.M. Wind: 52 mph North: 24° West: 63°	22 August, 1 A.M. Wind: 69 mph North: 26° West: 67°	23 August, 1 A.M. Wind: 121 mph North: 26° West: 73°

5	6	7	8
23 August, 1 P.M. Wind: 155 mph North: 25° West: 77°	24 August, 1 A.M. Wind: 138 mph North: 25° West: 79°	24 August, 7 A.M. Wind: 127 mph North: 26° West: 81°	24 August 1 P.M. Wind: 132 mph North: 26° West: 83°

9	10	11	12
25 August, 7 A.M. Wind: 132 mph North: 27° West: 88°	25 August, 7 P.M. Wind: 138 mph North: 29° West: 91°	26 August, 7 A.M. Wind: 92 mph North: 30° West: 92°	27 August, 1 A.M. Wind: 35 mph North: 32° West: 91°

The Wow's and Why's of Weather Scholastic Professional Books

Plot Andrew's Path of Destruction

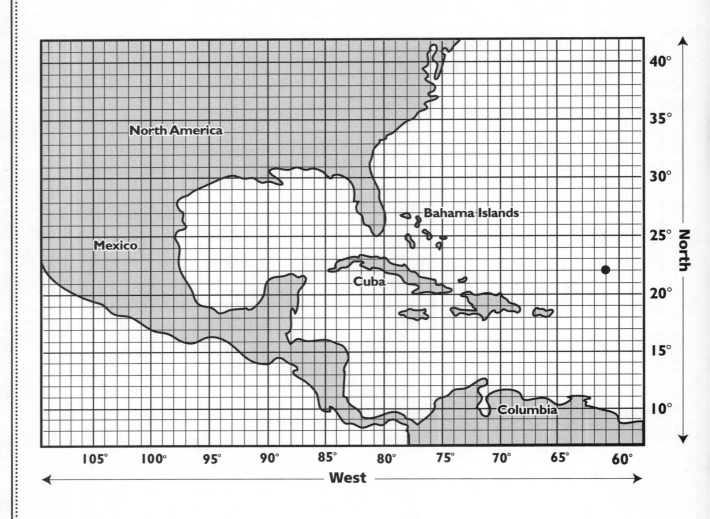

CHAPTER : 2

The Sun and the Seasons

Solar-Powered Weather

All weather on our planet is fueled by the sun—a medium-sized and middle-aged star of average brightness powered by the nuclear fusion of hydrogen into helium. It bathes the earth in solar energy, including light and heat.

But the earth is not evenly heated by the sun's energy. Differences in terrain, location on the globe, and the seasons result in an uneven heating of the earth's surfaces and subsequently the atmosphere above them. On a given day the equator bakes while the poles freeze, for example. Likewise a mountain town is much cooler than its valley neighbor. These global and local differences in hot and cold drive the weather engine on our planet by creating air masses of different temperatures which are the basis for pressure systems, fronts, and wind.

The Seasons and Temperature

Earth rotates on a tilted axis. That's why we have seasons. If Earth rotated in an upright position, all latitudes would have constant weather year-round. But because of the tilt, the Northern and Southern Hemispheres receive different amounts of sunlight during the year.

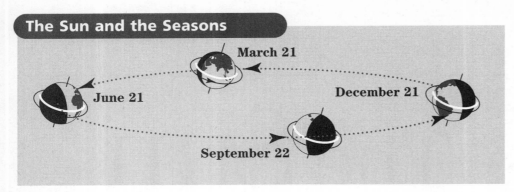

March 21

June 21

December 21

September 22

The Northern Hemisphere is tilted toward the sun during the summer which means that the sun rises high in the sky, shining its light directly down on the surface—greatly heating it. In contrast, during winter the Northern Hemisphere is tilted away from the sun, so the sun is low in the sky and its light reaches the surface at an indirect angle which spreads it out over a greater area. The light is less concentrated so it heats less. (This is easily seen by holding a flashlight at direct and indirect angles on a globe.) In addition, because the sun's arc is so low in the sky during winter, it makes a much shorter path. This is why the day is shorter, which means even less exposure to sunlight.

Temperature is the measure of how hot the air is. More accurately, it's a measure of the speed at which air molecules are moving. The faster the molecules, the higher the temperature. The temperature on the earth's surface averages about 59°F (15°C) at sea level. However, it can range from about -130 to 140°F (-88 to 58°C) depending on the season, latitude, elevation, and time of day. The hottest time of day is usually mid-afternoon, and the coldest is around dawn. The terrain greatly affects temperature because soil, water, and vegetation all absorb and give up heat at different rates. Land cools and warms quickly, whereas water doesn't.

So a lake's water can remain chilly even if its sandy beach is scorching hot. Dark areas absorb more heat than light areas, too. Areas covered in dark rock absorb heat and warm up, while a white snow-covered hill reflects sunlight and remains cool, for example.

Light is most concentrated from overhead source.

Light hitting at an angle is less concentrated.

Air Masses

Sunlight heats the land and water which in turn heat the air above them. When air stays over an area of land or water for many days, it tends to stabilize to an even temperature and humidity based on how cold, warm, dry, or wet the land below it is. This air becomes an air mass, a chunk of atmosphere that has a uniform temperature and humidity. Air masses are huge, often the size of two states. Most warm air masses form in the tropics and most cold ones at high latitudes. (It's difficult for air masses to form in the middle latitudes where air doesn't stay in one place very long.) Cold air masses move away from the poles toward warmer areas, and warm air masses move away from the tropics toward cooler areas. This is how the earth balances its "heat budget" to keep the poles from getting continually colder and the tropics from getting continually warmer. (Global ocean currents also help balance the heat budget.) Whether or not the air masses are wet or dry depends on where they formed—over water or land.

The four basic types of air masses are maritime tropical (wet and warm), maritime polar (wet and cold), continental tropical (dry and warm), and continental polar (dry and cold). When these air masses leave their area of origin, they bring rain, heat waves, cold spells, and storms along their path. The back-and-forth movement of hot and cold air masses—and the moisture and winds that goes with them—causes weather.

Storm Science: MONSOONS

The monsoons are a seasonal wind that bring rain by carrying moist ocean air in toward land. The word *monsoon* comes from the Arabic word for season, *mausim.* Monsoon rains fall in many areas of the tropics and subtropics including parts of northeast Australia, East Africa, the Caribbean, South America, and the southeastern United States. However, the Asian monsoons are the most extreme.

From October to April most of India is dry and dusty. Dry winter air over the cooling land sinks down on Asia, creating a large high-pressure area over the continent. Air moves from the high pressure over the continent to lower pressure over the Indian Ocean, creating dry winter winds that blow off the continent toward the water. But because of the seasonal tilt of Earth, in late April or May the land begins to heat from more direct sunlight. The air above the land heats up much faster than the air above the slower-warming ocean. Atmospheric pressure over the continent falls as it warms. Now air moves in from the cooler and higher–pressure ocean to replace the rising air mass over the warm land. The wind directions have switched, and they now bring moisture-laden air off the ocean that rains out in drenching storms as the air moves up toward the Himalayan mountains.

The monsoons bring a lot of rain. The rains brought by monsoons are the only rains some regions get all year. Nearly half of the world's population depends on monsoon rains to irrigate crops.

Weather and the Environment

GLOBAL CLIMATE CHANGE

When the earth's surface is warmed by the sun, gases in the atmosphere absorb and radiate back that heat. The gases act like an insulating coat or blanket that traps body heat. Take away the atmosphere and the earth's average temperature would fall from its current 60°F to about 0°F. This is called the greenhouse effect.

The "greenhouse gases" that absorb and radiate heat back to Earth make our planet habitable. The most common greenhouse gas is water vapor. Others include carbon dioxide, methane, nitrous oxide, and chloroflourocarbons (CFCs). Though many of these greenhouse gases occur naturally, their concentrations have increased over the past 100 years as humans burn fossil fuels and pollute.

With more greenhouse gases in the atmosphere, there is an enhanced greenhouse effect—the earth is additionally warmed by the denser blanket of gases. This is called global warming, or more accurately global climate change, because as the earth's overall temperature increases, some areas may warm while others may actually cool. It's estimated that there's been a mean rise in temperature of about 1.8°F (1°C) since 1850. A United Nations panel of scientists predicts an expected rise of another 6°F (3.3°C) in the next century if greenhouse gas emissions aren't reduced.

A few degrees warmer may not seem like much to worry about, but a rise of 3.6°F (2°C) means that sea level will likely rise 20 inches (51 cm) from melting ice caps and the expansion of water as it warms. Many coastal cities would flood, if not be completely destroyed, and some low-lying islands could eventually disappear.

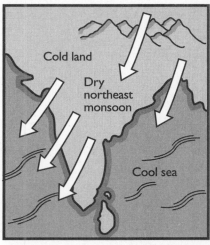

Dry Northeast Monsoon (October-April)

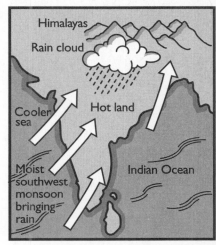

Wet Southwest Monsoon (May-September)

Fast Fact

The name *greenhouse effect* is something of a misnomer because greenhouses aren't warmed by exactly the same effect. (The air inside a greenhouse stays warm not from heat radiation, but because the glass traps in sun-warmed air).

Earth Systems Scientist

BRIAN O'NEILL

B rian O'Neill's job is predicting the future—the future of the earth's climate, that is. Scientists estimate that our planet's temperature has risen about 1.8°F (1°C) due to global climate change. The temperature will likely continue to rise as our growing world emits increasing amounts of greenhouse gases.

But exactly what a warmer earth will be like is unknown. What will the growing season be like in Russia? How much will the sea level rise by 2050? Can we solve the problem with cleaner cars or factories? "What if the United States reduces greenhouse gas emissions?" asks O'Neill. "How much better off would the climate be?"

These are questions that O'Neill and other scientists are trying to answer. He's an Earth Systems scientist at Brown University. So how does he find the answers to these questions? His "crystal ball" is the computer. Information collected about the earth's past climate as well as current conditions are processed by powerful data-crunching computers to model what might happen in the future.

O'Neill's job is a real challenge. Collecting information about the earth's climate isn't easy. The amount of carbon dioxide in the air is influenced by ocean currents, forest size, ocean chemistry, and atmospheric conditions, as well as how much pollution people make. But that's what keeps O'Neill fascinated. "Global climate change is connected to the whole history of the planet. This is the same system that's kept life around for billions of years and taken us in and out of ice ages," says O'Neill.

What do the computers tell O'Neill about the global climate? Computer modeling like this can predict what the climatic conditions on the earth would be like if emissions of greenhouse gases were reduced. The modeling also allows scientists to pinpoint how best to deal with the problem. Thanks to Brian O'Neill and other scientists like him, we can all prepare for a better future.

Photo courtesy of Brian O'Neill

Full of Hot Air

AIR MASSES

Air masses and the fronts their collisions create are an important part of understanding how weather is generated. The following activity will allow students to discover for themselves what happens when air is heated. As air heats up, its molecules move faster and spread out—the hot air expands. Then the hot air rises, because hot air is less dense, or lighter, than cold air. In this simple activity, students can easily see the expansion of hot air.

Directions

1 Fill one dish about halfway with cold tap water. Put a few ice cubes in it.

2 Put an inch or so of weights (marbles, pennies, etc.) in the bottle. Test the bottle to see if it floats by setting it in the dish of water. If it does float, add more weights.

3 Cap the bottle with a small balloon. (Be careful not to tear a hole in the balloon.)

4 Fill the other dish halfway with hot tap water. Set the balloon-topped bottle in the dish of hot water. Ask: *What happens? Why?* (The balloon inflates because as the air inside the bottle heats, the air expands.)

5 Once the balloon has popped up, move it to the dish of cold water. Ask: *What happens now? Why?* (The balloon collapses as the air inside the bottle cools and shrinks.) Help students connect the concept of hot air expanding to density by asking: *When was the air less dense—when it was cold or hot?* (hot) *Which is lighter, cold or hot air?* (hot)

Materials
(for the whole class)

small bottle with a narrow opening

small balloon

cold water

hot water

ice

two flat-bottomed dishes or containers

marbles, pennies, sand, or pebbles (anything to add weight to the bottle)

Note: The bigger the bottle and the balloon, the more extreme the differences in hot and cold need to be, which is why a small bottle and balloon are recommended. If you want to use a large bottle and balloon, use a glass bottle and set it in a pan of heated water. Then use oven mitts to carefully move the bottle to a bowl of ice.

Build a Weather Station

THERMOMETER

Students can measure and monitor changes in temperature with this fun-to-make thermometer. It works on the same principle as a real thermometer. The liquid (water) expands as it heats up, forcing its way up the straw.

Note that the scale used to measure the temperature on these thermometers is not a Celsius or Fahrenheit scale, but a simple scale designed to illustrate the basic principle of temperatures rising and falling. If you wish, you can help students calibrate their thermometers using a Celsius or Fahrenheit thermometer. Another thing to remember is that the units on the scale will not be accurate at or below freezing because water expands when frozen.

Materials

(for each group)

16-oz. glass bottle

two white or clear straws

water

food coloring

modeling clay

reproducible pages 29 and 30

glue

index card

baby oil (optional)

Instrument of Interest: The Thermometer

A thermometer measures temperature. Galileo is usually credited with its invention around 1592. More modern alcohol and mercury thermometers were invented by German physicist Gabriel Fahrenheit in 1714. They work on the principle of a liquid expanding and rising in a tube that is sealed on both ends. Fahrenheit also developed the standardized scale of temperature named after him in which water boils at 212° and freezes at 32°. The Celsius temperature scale (or °C) was created in 1742 by Swedish astronomer Anders Celsius. In the Celsius scale, water freezes at 0° and boils at 100°.

Directions

Divide the class into three or four groups. Have them follow these instructions:

1 Roll the clay into a ball. Its diameter needs to be slightly larger than the mouth of the bottle.

2 Set the clay ball on a table or desk. Use one of the straws to poke a hole through the center of the ball of clay. Try to make the hole as straight and as clean as you can. Once the hole goes completely through the clay ball, pull the straw out.

3 Carefully push a new straw into the hole made in step 2. Push it until about two inches of straw is sticking out of the bottom of the clay. Pinch and pat the clay around the straw on both sides to make a tight seal.

4 Fill the bottle to the top with room-temperature water and add a few drops of food coloring (so the water is easier to see as it travels up the straw.)

5 Place the longer end of the straw into the bottle. Firmly press down on the ball of clay at the bottle's mouth to make an airtight seal. Colored water should rise up into the straw beyond the mouth of the bottle. If it doesn't, just pour a little extra colored water into the straw. If the water doesn't stay in the straw, there is a leak in the seal that needs to be resealed. (Hint: If you'll be using the thermometers for a few days, this is a good time to add a drop of clear baby oil into the straw to prevent evaporation.)

6 Glue the scale on page 29 onto an index card and cut it out. Carefully slide the card into the clay just behind the straw. A little glue will help keep it there.

7 Cut out the label on page 29, wrap it around the front of the bottle, and secure with tape.

8 Record the date, time, and temperature reading on the chart on page 30. (Note: If there's added baby oil in the straw, instruct students to read where the colored water ends.) The water level will rise and fall as it contracts and expands in response to changes in temperature. Monitor the room temperature for change over time, recording your observations on the chart.

Extensions

• The changes in room temperature will be very slight on students' thermometers. Consider allowing students to place their thermometers in some "extreme" conditions such as in the refrigerator or near a heat vent or sunny window.

• Challenge student groups to investigate how animals are adapted to different temperatures in their habitats. For example, how are polar bears adapted to the cold? camels to the desert?

Fast Fact

Some kinds of crickets are a fairly accurate thermometer. Just count the number of chirps one of these crickets makes in 14 seconds and add 40 to get degrees Fahrenheit.

ACTIVITY

Monsoon Map

STORM SCIENCE: MONSOONS

The Asian monsoons of India are the world's most extreme—and famous—of these kinds of storms. But seasonal monsoon rains are an important part of the yearly rainfall of many countries besides India. In this map-reading activity, students will learn where monsoon winds switch and bring rain as the seasons change.

Photocopy and distribute page 31 to students. Explain that the shaded areas show where monsoons occur. Tell students to use the map to answer the questions.

Answers: 1. Antarctica and Europe 2. Ethiopia 3. Atlantic Ocean, Indian Ocean, Pacific Ocean 4. Australia 5. the Southeast

Materials
(for each group)

reproducible page 31

Hothouse Heat-Up

Weather and the Environment: GLOBAL CLIMATE CHANGE

In this activity, students discover how the greenhouse effect causes global warming when they use plastic wrap to represent the heat-trapping greenhouse gases in the atmosphere.

Note: This experiment is not a perfect model for how the atmosphere traps heat since the mechanism for trapping is a barrier—the plastic wrap—instead of gases that absorb heat and radiate it back.

Directions

Divide the class into pairs and provide each pair with a set of materials and a copy of page 32. Decide as a class which unit of temperature you'll use (Fahrenheit or Celsius). Then have students follow these directions:

1 Fill the cartons with two cups of soil each. Cover the top of one soil-filled carton with plastic wrap; make sure the wrap is stretched tightly over the top.

2 Place a thermometer in each container. (Poke the thermometer through the plastic wrap on the second container of soil.) The thermometers need to go into the soil, not lay on top.

3 Choose a different colored pencil to keep records for each container. Note the starting time on your sheet and record a starting temperature for both containers on the 0 minutes line.

4 Set the containers under a lamp. Make sure both containers are equally exposed to the light. They can be close together, but shouldn't touch.

5 Add five minutes onto the starting time and write that time under the 5 minutes line. (Students can do this all the way across to help them know when it's time to take temperatures). Take the temperature of the containers at 5, 10, and 15 minutes from the start time. Plot each container's temperature in its color on the graph. (You may want to encourage one student in the pair to be the temperature reader and the other to be the recorder.)

6 After 15 minutes, turn off the lamp. (This is a good time for partners to switch jobs.) Continue to record the temperatures at 20, 25, and 30 minutes.

7 When all the data has been recorded, carefully connect the points using the colored pencils. You should end up with four different colored graph lines. Use the data to answer the questions on your paper.

8 Answer the questions at the bottom of the page. Compare the slopes of the lines of the graphs to find your answers.

Materials

(for each pair)

two milk cartons with tops cut off (any identical containers that hold water will do)

dark potting soil

plastic wrap

two thermometers (hanging aquarium thermometers work well)

lamp

colored pens or pencils

reproducible page 32

watch or clock

Note: You'll want to set the soil, in the room ahead of time so it reaches room temperature.

Answers: 1. soil covered with plastic 2. soil 3. soil covered with plastic 4. soil Bonus: The plastic wrap acted like a barrier, trapping the warm air inside.

Make a Thermometer

Cut out the label.

Tape the label to the bottle.
Attach the scale to a card
and slide it into the clay ball.

Thermometer
(thuh-MOM-uh-ter)
measures temperature

WARMER

10
9
8
7
6
5
4
3
2
1
0

10
9
8
7
6
5
4
3
2
1
0

COOLER

The Wow's and Why's of Weather Scholastic Professional Books

Make a Thermometer

Date	Time	Temperature Reading	Where is the thermometer?

The Wow's and Why's of Weather Scholastic Professional Books

Name_____

Monsoon Countries

Monsoons are strong winds that change with the seasons and bring downpours to parts of the world. Monsoons occur in the shaded areas on this map. Use the map to answer the questions below.

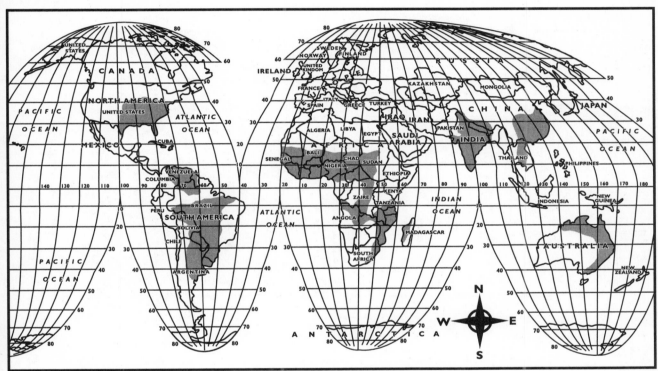

Questions

1 What two of the seven continents have no monsoons?_____

2 Which of these African countries does NOT have monsoons?
(circle one)   Nigeria   Ethiopia   Senegal

3 Monsoon rains start over the ocean. Name three oceans over which monsoon rains might start. _____

4 Are you more likely to experience a monsoon in Canada, Peru, or Australia?

_____

5 Which part of the United States gets monsoons?
(circle one)   the Southeast   the Northeast   the Northwest

The Wow's and Why's of Weather Scholastic Professional Books

Name _____

Hothouse Heat-Up

Use this sheet to record the results of your experiment.
Color in the boxes in the key with the pens you'll use to draw each line on the graph.

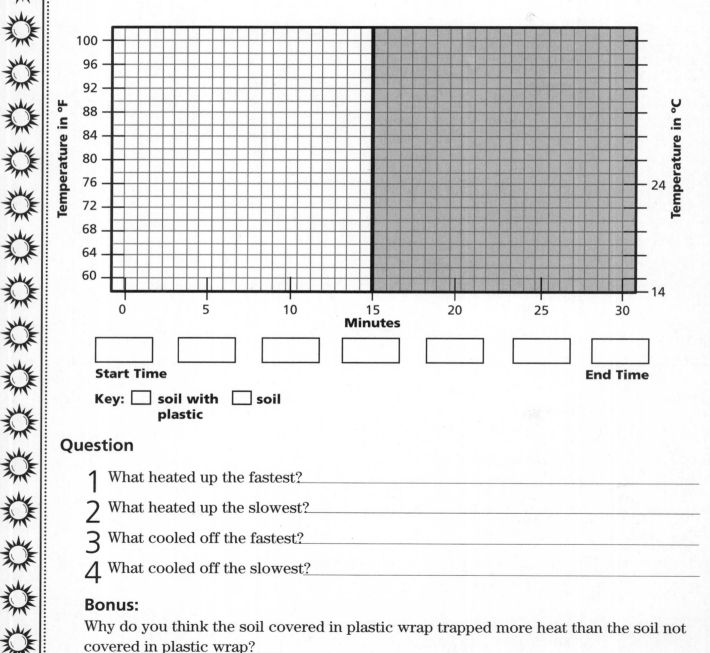

Key: ☐ soil with plastic   ☐ soil

Question

1 What heated up the fastest? _____

2 What heated up the slowest? _____

3 What cooled off the fastest? _____

4 What cooled off the slowest? _____

Bonus:

Why do you think the soil covered in plastic wrap trapped more heat than the soil not covered in plastic wrap? _____

32

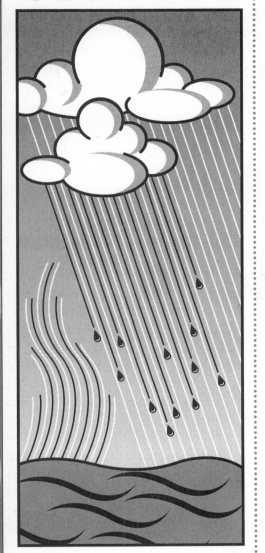

CHAPTER 3

Clouds and Rain

The Water Cycle

We live on a watery planet. Ocean alone covers more than 70 percent of the surface of the earth. Added to that is the water in rivers, lakes, streams, and ponds, and the ice at the poles. Even the air around us—the atmosphere—contains an enormous amount of water in the form of water vapor, a gas.

The continuous movement of water back and forth between the earth's surface and the atmosphere is called the water cycle. It involves water changing phase from a liquid to a gas and back to a liquid. Heated liquid water changes into water vapor during evaporation (the transition of a liquid to a gas). As the water vapor rises, it cools, and the molecules of water form droplets. This is called condensation (the transition of a gas to a liquid), or sublimation (the transition of a gas to a solid) if it's cold enough to form ice crystals. Water vapor condensing into tiny droplets around dust, smoke, or other condensation nuclei creates clouds. If the droplets grow too large and heavy to be held up by air currents, they fall to the ground as precipitation.

The type of precipitation that falls depends on its size, the temperature of the cloud, and the temperature of the air on the way down. Drizzle, for example, is made up of drops smaller than .02 inches (.5 mm) in diameter, whereas rain is liquid precipitation larger than .02 inches (.5 mm). Freezing rain falls to the ground as water and freezes into ice on contact with any surface, whereas sleet is made of raindrops that have frozen in midair.

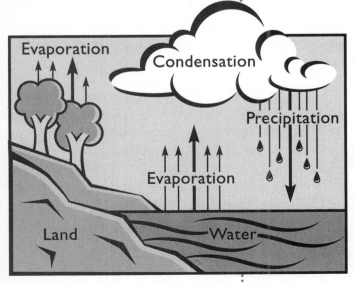

Snow is made up of ice crystals that formed as cloud droplets froze. Hailstones are balls of ice that are usually formed from clusters of raindrops frozen in thunderstorm updrafts. Fog is simply a cloud at ground level.

What causes water to change form? It's all about cooling and heating. Cooling changes water vapor to a liquid or solid; it also changes liquid water to ice. When water cools, it adds heat to the surrounding air. On the other hand, changing ice to vapor or liquid, or liquid to vapor, requires added heat. That heat is taken from surrounding air, leaving the air cooled. The heat that water adds and subtracts from surrounding air when it changes phase is called latent heat and plays a big part in fueling storms.

Humidity and Dew Point

Humidity is how much water vapor is in the air. All air holds some water vapor, even dry desert air. The amount of water vapor that air can hold depends on the temperature. Cold air can hold less water vapor than warm air before that water vapor condenses and forms a liquid. The faster-moving molecules in warm air mean that more water can remain as vapor without being condensed into liquid. Air's capacity to hold water vapor roughly doubles with each temperature increase of 10°C. The temperature at which air loses its ability to hold water vapor (is saturated), and condensation occurs, is the dew point. It's the temperature of the air when dew—water vapor condensing to liquid—forms. If the dew point temperature is below freezing, frost forms.

The amount of water vapor in the air is referred to in two different ways. Meteorologists want to know the specific humidity, or the actual amount of water in the air, which is usually measured in parts per thousand. Weather reporters, however, usually talk about the relative humidity. Relative humidity is the specific humidity divided by the vapor-holding capacity of air at a given temperature. A relative humidity reading of 75 percent means that the air contains 75 percent of the water vapor it can possibly hold for that particular temperature. Although the specific humidity might not change all day, the relative humidity will change as the temperature rises and falls.

Clouds

Clouds are made of tiny water droplets and/or ice crystals suspended by air and updrafts. This is possible because the water droplets in clouds are very small—it takes a million cloud drops to make a single raindrop. When cloud droplets or ice crystals grow large enough, they fall as precipitation. Clouds are classified into many different identifiable types. The names of clouds are made up of Latin words that describe their general shape and often the height at which they are found. Most cloud

Cloud Types

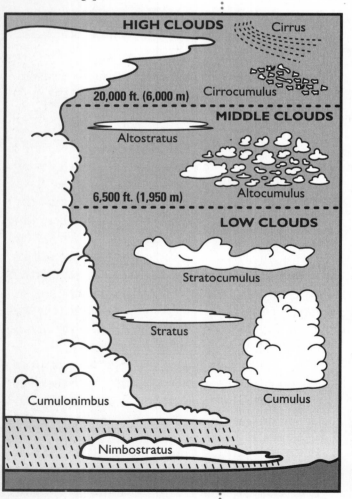

HIGH CLOUDS — Cirrus

Cirrocumulus

20,000 ft. (6,000 m)

MIDDLE CLOUDS

Altostratus

Altocumulus

6,500 ft. (1,950 m)

LOW CLOUDS

Stratocumulus

Stratus

Cumulonimbus

Cumulus

Nimbostratus

names are one of three cloud shapes—cirrus, stratus, and cumulus. Cirrus are curly or stringy-looking clouds made of ice crystals. Stratus clouds are stratified, or layered, and flat. Cumulus are lumpy, fluffy, often piled-up clouds. The shape name can be combined with a word such as *cirro, alto*, and *nimbo*. *Cirro-* means the cloud is high, with a base above 20,000 feet (6,000 meters) or so. *Alto-* means mid-level, or about 6,000 to 20,000 feet (1,800-6,000 meters). There is no prefix for low. The prefix or suffix *nimbo* means the cloud is making precipitation. Therefore, a cirrocumulus is a high, fluffy cloud, whereas a cumulonimbus is a fluffy rain-making cloud. One exception to the cloud-naming rule is the stratocumulus cloud; it's made up of two shape words, because it looks both fluffy and layered.

Because clouds are made of "weather," they give insight into what the weather is like—and what's on the way. For example, nimbostratus clouds usually mean that rain or snow is coming, whereas cumulus clouds (that don't grow larger) mean a clear day. You can't predict the weather by simply by studying the cloud types in the sky, but they are an important tool.

Storm Science: THUNDERSTORMS AND LIGHTNING

Our planet experiences as many as 50,000 thunderstorms every day. They are the world's most common kind of storm, bringing drenching rain, hail, lightning and thunder, and sometimes spawning tornadoes (see page 52). In North America, most thunderstorms happen in the spring and summer. That's when air near the ground is warm but air aloft is cold. These unstable air conditions spawn the giant anvil-shaped cumulonimbus clouds that produce thunderstorms. As the warm, moist air rises off the ground, as an updraft, it begins to cool. Once it reaches its dew point temperature, a cloud begins to form. The condensation process that forms the cloud warms the air, allowing the cloud to continue to rise if conditions are right. This is how the tall, vertical, towering shape of the thunderhead develops.

Inside the cloud, updrafts keep pumping warm, humid air into the storm—further fueling it. Meanwhile, some ice and water droplets grow large enough to fall out, dragging air down with them and creating downdrafts. The updrafts and downdrafts zoom up and down the cloud as fast as 5,000 feet (1,500 meters) per minute. Ice caught in the updrafts can be recirculated, adding layer upon layer of ice until it falls out as hail.

One of the dangerous results of thunderstorms is lightning. Lightning happens when electricity travels between negatively and positively charged parts of a cloud or between a cloud and the ground. Lightning is how a charged cloud "dumps" its charge. How a cloud becomes charged isn't completely known. Scientists think the chaotic mix of updrafts and downdrafts that zip around inside a thunderhead may

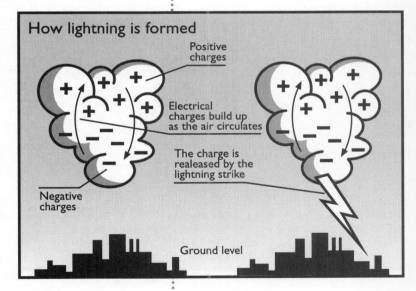

How lightning is formed

Positive charges

Electrical charges build up as the air circulates

The charge is realeased by the lightning strike

Negative charges

Ground level

cause it. Updrafts carry some water upward where it becomes ice; other water in the cloud exists as liquid. This may cause different sections of the cloud to have different charges.

When a cloud discharges and lightning flashes, it heats the air to more than 43,000°F (23,871°C) along its path. That air expands and immediately contracts because the lightning is moving so fast—60,000 miles (96,000 km) per second. The quick expansion and contraction of the air creates sound waves, called thunder. Sound travels much slower than light, so we see the flash and then hear the thunder.

Weather and the Environment
ACID RAIN

The pH of normal rainwater is slightly acidic because of the carbon dioxide dissolved in it. However, certain air pollutants can make rainwater extra acidic, which is then called acid rain. Acid rain can damage forests and crops; make ponds, streams, and lakes unable to support life; and destroy buildings and statues.

Acid rain is formed when the smoke and fumes from burning fossil fuels such as oil, coal, and gasoline rise in the atmosphere, emitting sulfur dioxide and nitrogen oxide. Usually up high in the clouds, these pollutants react and form mild sulfuric and nitric acid solutions. When the clouds form precipitation—such as snow, rain, or fog—the acids are carried with them back down to the earth. (Acids from pollutants that don't make it into clouds also fall back to the earth as dry particles and gases.) Because clouds can travel many hundreds of miles before "raining out" their acids, acid rain can fall far from its source.

Acid rain affects both plant and animal life in land and water ecosystems. Trees exposed to acid rain—or dry acid deposits—are weakened and can have stunted growth. Leaves burned by the acids are unable to photosynthesize food. Scientists also believe that acidic water leeches needed nutrients and minerals from the soil. Lakes, streams, and ponds often take the brunt of acid rain because they not only collect the acid rain that falls directly into them, but also take in acid rain and dry acid deposits that enter as runoff. The result can be disastrous—fish eggs and insect larvae won't hatch, the aquatic food web begins to disintegrate, and in very extreme cases the pond or lake will die.

Is there a solution? In 1988, 25 countries—including the U.S.—agreed to hold nitrogen oxide emissions at 1987 levels. In the United States, the 1990 amendments to the Clean Air Act call for power plants to reduce their emission of sulfur dioxide 10 million tons per year by the year 2000.

Storm Photographer

WARREN FAIDLEY

Warren Faidley is the world's only full-time, professional storm photographer. His award-winning photographs have appeared in magazines, newspapers, and books. He was a consultant for the blockbuster movie *Twister,* too. Faidley stalks and shoots about one hundred storms a year—midwest tornadoes in the spring, southwest lightning storms in the summer, and Atlantic hurricanes in the late summer and fall.

Photographing lightning and snapping hurricane images can be treacherous at times. "Lightning that hit near me launched my career," explains Faidley. He was taking pictures in Arizona when a lightning bolt struck a light pole only 400 feet (122 meters) away. The flash blinded him, and he fell down an embankment—but the photograph made *Life* magazine.

Since then, Faidley has waited around for lightning to strike twice. He actively searches for storms in a vehicle outfitted with communications, computer, and weather-forecasting equipment to help him find photogenic storms and weather. Though not a trained meteorologist—he studied journalism in college—Faidley has learned a lot about how to use weather data to forecast what's on the way. "We do most of our own forecasting because we're looking for specific storms in a very targeted area," explains Faidley. "We use the same things as the weather service—dew point, winds, and barometric pressure."

Warren Faidley
**http://www.
stormchaser.com/**

Visit Faidley's site to see some of his spectacular storm photos for yourself.

Cycling Water & Heat

THE WATER CYCLE

Materials

(for the whole class)

glass loaf pan or clear plastic food container, with clear lid

small bowl

warm water

ice cubes

plastic bag that closes

strong lamp

The water cycle is an important concept for students studying weather because it explains the formation of clouds and precipitation. It's also a great opportunity for students to learn about phase or state changes of water and to understand the concept of latent heat absorption and release that drives storms. In this activity students create and observe a mini-water cycle that goes through evaporation, condensation, and precipitation.

Directions

1 Set the bowl inside the container at one end. Fill the bowl with warm tap water. This is your "lake." Close the lid.

2 Put the lamp a few inches over the container's lid directly over the bowl of water. The lamp is the "sun." Turn the sun on and let it shine over the lake for two hours. After two hours, ask: *What happened?* (Some of the water in the bowl has evaporated.) *Where is the water?* (It's in the air inside of the container, and some condensed into drops inside the lid.) Note: This is a great time to review evaporation, condensation, and phase changes! Consider asking students if latent heat was released or absorbed during evaporation. (It is absorbed.)

3 Put ice cubes into the plastic bag and close it. Set the bag of ice on top of the lid at the opposite end as the lamp. Leave the lamp on and wait another two hours. Ask: *What happens?* (It rained.) *Why?* (The cooling ice made the temperature drop, and water vapor in the air condensed into rain.) *Did you observe clouds in the meantime? Why?* (The water vapor in the air first condensed into clouds before condensing into raindrops.) Consider asking students if latent heat was released or absorbed during condensation. (It was released.)

Extension

Students can measure the heat released and absorbed when water changes phase. Have students wrap the bulb of a thermometer in a piece of cloth and note the temperature. Then wet the cloth on the thermometer, wave it in the air to help the water evaporate, and read the temperature again. How many degrees of heat were lost during evaporation? Where did that heat go? (It released into the air when the liquid water changed to water vapor.) The reverse can also be seen by placing two thermometers in the freezer—one on top of a water-filled ice cube tray and the other off to the side. Read the thermometers every ten minutes and compare. How many degrees of heat were gained during the water freezing? Where did they go? (They were released into the surrounding air.)

Cloud Key

I dentifying clouds is a terrific way for students to put their skills of observation and classification to work, as well as to launch them into weather
prediction. Clouds are only one of the many factors—including fronts, winds,
pressure systems, etc.—that contribute to predicting weather, but they are
one that students can easily observe. Note: Identifying clouds can be difficult
at first. Encourage students to make their best guesses based on the dominant
kind of clouds they see, or to list more than one type.

Materials
(for each student)

**reproducible pages
45 and 46**

brass paper fastener

scissors

Directions

1 Make a copy of the reproducible for each student. Show students how to make
the Cloud Key by cutting out both circles on pages 45 and 46, cutting out and
discarding the two shaded areas on page 45, and fastening the wheels together. Page 45 goes on top.

2 Show students how to use the key. Move the wheel until the
cloud you want appears, then read the name and weather
information in the box.

3 Have students make a chart with these five headings:
"Date/Time," "Cloud Type," "A.M. Weather," "P.M. Predicted
Weather," "Actual P.M. Weather/Time." (See the sample
shown here.) Invite students to fill in the chart every morning for a week, comparing their predictions to the actual
weather in the afternoon.

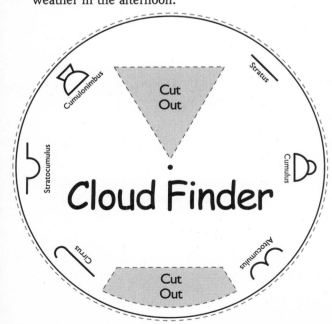

Date/ Time	Cloud Type	AM Weather	Predicted Weather PM	Weather/ Time

Mapping Out Rain & Snow

PRECIPITATION PATTERNS

Precipitation is any form of moisture that falls out of clouds—snow, rain, hail, sleet, etc. U.S. meteorologists measure and track annual precipitation in inches of liquid. So even though snowfall is recorded in inches of depth, it's added into a region's annual precipitation in terms of how much water it would make. In general there's a 1:10 ratio for rain to snow.

Materials

(for each student)

reproducible pages 47 and 48

map of the USA

Answers: 1. Michigan; Minnesota 2. same 3. Colorado; at least 6 inches 4. Florida, Alabama, or Mississippi 5. Arizona 6. and Bonus: Answers will vary

Directions

Reproduce pages 47 and 48 and distribute both to students. Review the term *precipitation* with students. Ask: *What does it include?* Go over what each map is showing—inches of snow and inches of overall precipitation—before allowing students to answer the questions on page 47 on their own. Give students access to a U.S. map to help them identify the states in the reproducible maps.

Do the Dew Point

DEW POINT

Glasses filled with cold drinks "sweat" because they cool the air immediately around them to the dew point—the temperature at which water vapor in the air condenses to liquid. (This is how clouds form.) The water droplets condense out of the air outside the cold glass. In this simple activity students will find the dew point temperature in the classroom.

Materials

(for class)

metal can with label and top removed

ice

room-temperature water

thermometer

Directions

1 Fill the can about halfway with room-temperature water. Make sure the outside of the can is dry.

2 Place the thermometer in the can and record the temperature. Leave the thermometer in the can.

3 Add a few ice cubes and stir. Carefully watch the outside of the can for "sweat" droplets to form. When they do, record the temperature. This is the dew point temperature.

4 Invite students to use steps 1-3 to measure dew points under different conditions of humidity and temperature—outside, in a steamy locker room, etc.

Build a Weather Station

R A I N   G A U G E

This rain gauge will allow your students to measure rainfall.

Directions

1. Carefully cut the plastic bottle where the sides start to slope up to the mouth. Put tape around both cut edges. The top will act as a funnel.

2. Place enough weights into the bottom of the large half of the bottle to stabilize it.

3. Set the funnel inside the bottle so the taped edges touch.

4. Cut out the scale on page 49 and tape it onto the outside of the bottle. Make sure the 0 line is above the weights and at a level where the bottle's shape is uniform. Use clear packing tape to completely cover the scale so it's waterproof.

5. Pour water into the gauge until it reaches the 0 line on the bottom of the scale. The gauge will need to be reset to this level each day that rainfall is to be measured.

6. Set the rain gauge outside in an open area, avoiding trees and building overhangs. Have students record rainfall and amounts on a chart.

Rain Gauge measures precipitation

Extension

If it's snowing in your area at this time of year, have students measure snowfall. Find a flat, level area on the ground and measure the snow that has accumulated there with a ruler. Students can use the equation 10 inches of snow = 1 inch of rain to convert the inches of snow to precipitation. Or they can determine their own conversion factor by letting a coffee can of the snow melt and then comparing the original amount of snow to the amount of water formed from the melted snow. What's their experimentally determined ratio?

Materials

(for class)

empty 1- or 2-liter plastic bottle

small weights (marbles, aquarium gravel, clean stones, or pennies work well)

scissors

clear packing tape

reproducible page 49

[ONLINE] LINK

National Weather Service Homepage http://www.nws. noaa.gov

How can you find out where it's raining or snowing anywhere in the world? Just visit this information-packed site! Students can use the site to hold Rainy Day Races: Each student picks a city somewhere in the country or the world and keeps track of the precipitation it receives for one week. The winning city is the one with the most rain or snow.

Build a Weather Station

PSYCHROMETER

Students can accurately measure relative humidity with this wet-and-dry bulb thermometer, or psychrometer.

Materials

(for class)

reproducible page 50

half-gallon plastic milk jug with lid

scissors

two Fahrenheit thermometers

cotton shoestring with tips cut off or a six-by-one-inch strip of absorbent cloth

rubber bands

permanent marker or grease pencil

Instrument of Interest: **The Psychrometer**

A psychrometer (si-CHROM-uh-ter) is an instrument used to measure relative humidity. It's often called a wet-and-dry bulb thermometer because it's made of two thermometers, one with a normal dry bulb and the other with a bulb wrapped in wet cloth. The wet-bulb thermometer is cooled by evaporation, the amount of which is dependent on the amount of water vapor in the air. (The drier the air, the faster the water will evaporate and the more the wet bulb will cool.) The difference between the two temperatures is used to calculate relative humidity using a table.

Directions

1 Carefully cut a dime-size hole about two inches from the bottom of the jug on one of the sides.

2 Wrap the bulb of one of the thermometers with one end of the shoestring and use a rubber band to secure it. It needs to have a three-inch "tail" remaining.

3 Thread the shoestring tail through the hole and use a rubber band to attach the thermometer to the outside of the carton. Write *WET BULB* above or below it.

4 Use another rubber band to attach the other thermometer to an adjacent side of the jug. Write *DRY BULB* above or below it.

5 Pour water into the jug until the shoelace soaks up water, but doesn't leak out the hole. Let the water and thermometers come to room temperature and make sure the shoelace is soaking up water. The shoestring around the bulb should feel wet.

6 Air needs to move past the wet bulb to insure an accurate reading. Ask students to fan the air around the wet-bulb thermometer using an old folder or piece of posterboard.

7 Have students record both the wet- and dry-bulb temperatures and use the table on page 50 to determine relative humidity. Then have them record the daily humidity on a chart by repeating steps 6 and 7. Challenge them to correlate humidity levels with coming or passing storms or rain.

Extension

Challenge students to measure the relative humidity in different rooms—such as steamy locker rooms, closets, a kitchen, or an auditorium—and compare findings.

Static Sensor

Storm Science: LIGHTNING

Lightning happens when positive and negative charges build up in separate parts of storm clouds. This buildup of extra charges is called static electricity. Your students experience small doses of static electricity when they walk across a carpet and are greeted by a zap when they touch a metal doorknob. Lightning is just static electricity on a *much* bigger scale. Students build an instrument to detect the static electric charge of an object. Note: This activity works best on dry days.

Directions

Divide the class into small groups. Then have students follow these instructions:

1 Make a "T" with the craft stick, pencil, and masking tape as shown.

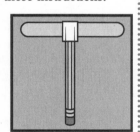

2 Tear off 2 three-inch strips of cellophane tape and attach them to the edge of a desk or table so that they dangle.

3 Write a – symbol on the smooth side about midway down on one and a + on the other strip.

4 Stick the sticky side of the + strip of tape onto the smooth side of the – strip and then quickly peel them apart.

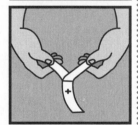

5 Stick one end of each tape strip onto an end of the craft stick so they dangle down. The strips' smooth and sticky sides should face the same way.

6 The Static Sensor is ready! Use a balloon rubbed on hair or wool to test it. Computer or TV screens also test well. The strip of tape that moves forward toward the object indicates if the charge is negative or positive. (A negatively charged object has more electrons than protons. A positively charged object has more protons than electrons.) If the strips do not move at all, then the object has no charge.

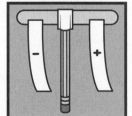

7 Challenge students to make predictions about the charge of various objects and then test them (no charge/positively charged/negatively charged). Have them record their predictions and results on a chart and then compare results.

Extension

In the United States about one hundred persons a year are killed by lightning—more than by tornadoes or hurricanes. Challenge groups of students to investigate lightning safety and create informative public safety posters.

Materials
(for each group)

unsharpened pencil

craft stick

Scotch Magic cellophane tape (Other kinds of clear tape work, but not all of them do. Test your kind before using.)

balloon

wool mitten, yarn, or hat

masking tape

pen or magic marker

Book Break

Lightning! And Thunderstorms by Mike Graf (Simon Spotlight, 1998) Students will want to record their own experiences with and memories of lightning after reading this book filled with fascinating accounts and photos.

Testing for Trouble

Weather and the Environment: ACID RAIN

Acid rain is caused by acidic chemical pollutants emitted into the air by cars, trucks, factories, and power plants. In this activity students make an acid/base indicator solution and test rainwater for acidity. Make sure your students are familiar with the terms *acid* and *base* and their meanings before doing the activity (see page 36).

Materials

(for the whole class)

medium-sized red cabbage

one quart distilled water

pan

stove, hot plate, or microwave

strainer

knife

vinegar

baking soda

collected rainwater

four small glasses or jars

measuring cups

tablespoon

Book Break

Acid Rain by Sally Morgan (Franklin Watts, 1999)

Is acid rain a problem where you live? After they read the book, challenge students to find newspaper and magazine articles in the library that discuss the problem in your area.

Directions

1 Wash and pat dry a red cabbage and then cut it up. Fill a pan with a quart of distilled water. Place the pieces of cabbage in the pan of water, cover it, and let it simmer for about 30 minutes. (Or cook it in a microwave for about 15 minutes.)

2 Set it aside and let it cool. Then strain the 2-3 cups of juice into a glass jar. This is your acid/base indicator. (Red cabbage juice can be used as a pH indicator because red cabbage contains a chemical that turns from its natural deep purple color to red in acids and blue in bases.)

3 Label the four glasses: "Water," "Rain," "Acid," "Base."

4 Fill the "Rain" glass with 1 cup of rainwater and set it aside.

5 Fill the other three glasses with 1 cup of distilled water. Add a tablespoon of vinegar to the "Acid" glass and a tablespoon of baking soda to the "Base" glass. Do nothing to the "Water" glass.

6 Now pour 1/4 cup of the indicator into each glass. Ask students to record and compare their results. Ask: *What color does the indicator turn for an acid?* (red) *a base?* (blue) *Is rainwater acidic, basic ,or neutral?* (probably a little bit acidic, or neutral) *Is it a strong or weak acid?* (probably weak)

Extension

Invite students to investigate the effects of acid rain on plant growth. Have them water one plant—such as a bean seedling or a cutting from a philodendron—with distilled water, and an identical plant with acidified water (add 1 teaspoon vinegar to 2 cups of water). Ask them to chart the plants' growth and record their observations of the plants' appearance over a period of weeks. (Consider digging up the plants and examining the roots at the end—this is where they'll see quite a difference.)

Cut out the wheel.
Cut out the two shaded areas inside the wheel.
This is the top wheel of your cloud key.

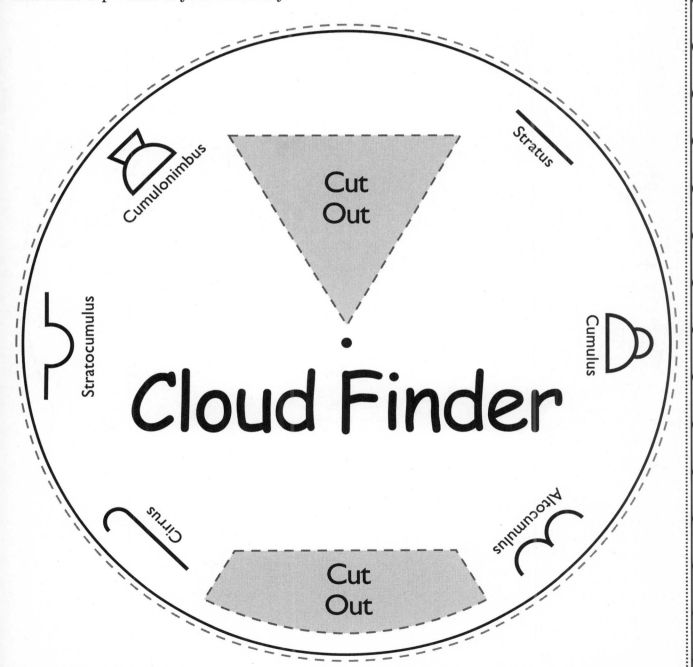

The Wow's and Why's of Weather Scholastic Professional Books

Cloud Finder

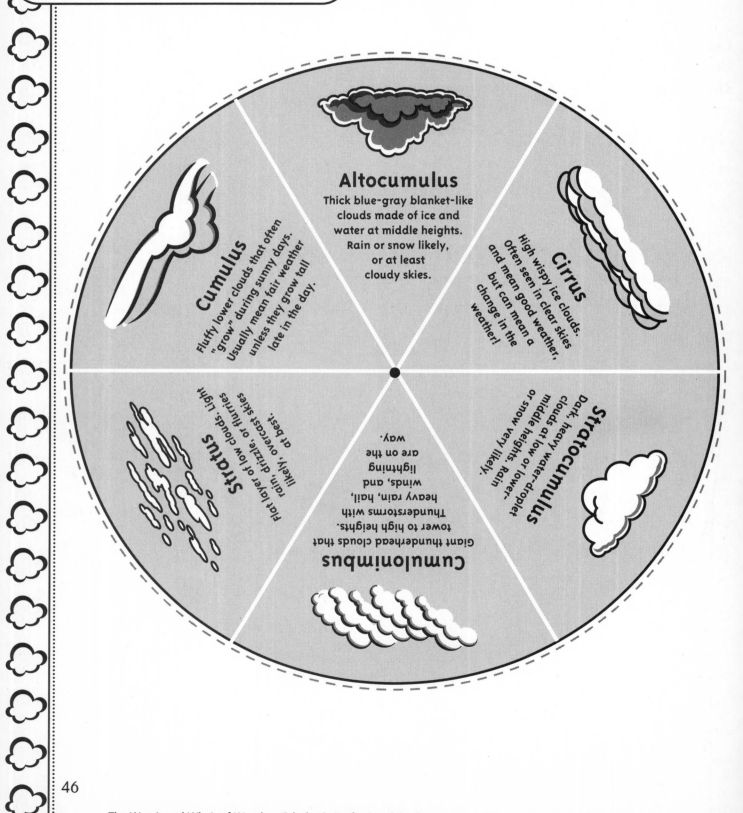

Altocumulus
Thick blue-gray blanket-like clouds made of ice and water at middle heights. Rain or snow likely, or at least cloudy skies.

Cirrus
High wispy ice clouds. Often seen in clear skies and mean good weather, but can mean a change in the weather!

Cumulus
Fluffy lower clouds that often "grow" during sunny days. Usually mean fair weather unless they grow tall late in the day.

Stratocumulus
Dark, heavy water-droplet clouds at low or lower-middle heights. Rain or snow very likely.

Stratus
Flat layer of low clouds. Light rain, drizzle, or flurries likely, overcast skies at best.

Cumulonimbus
Giant thunderhead clouds that tower to high heights. Thunderstorms with heavy rain, hail, winds, and lightning are on the way.

The Wow's and Why's of Weather Scholastic Professional Books

Name_____

Mapping Out Rain and Snow

Use the maps on page 48 to answer the questions below.

Questions

1 Which state gets more snow—Michigan or Minnesota?_____

Which of the two gets more overall precipitation?_____

2 Which state gets more overall precipitation per year—Maine or Illinois?

_____

3 What state gets more than 60 inches of snow, but less than 16 inches of overall
precipitation? (circle one)   Colorado   Iowa   Pennsylvania

At least how many inches of this state's total precipitation comes from snow?

_____

4 Name a state that gets less than 1 inch of snow, but more than 48 inches of rain each year.

_____

5 What state gets less than 16 inches of overall precipitation in most areas and less than
an inch of snow each year? (circle one)   Montana   Arizona   Utah

6 What's the average annual snowfall where you live?_____

annual overall precipitation?_____

Bonus:
About how much of your annual precipitation is snow? _____

_____

The Wow's and Why's of Weather Scholastic Professional Books

Name _____

Mapping Out Rain and Snow

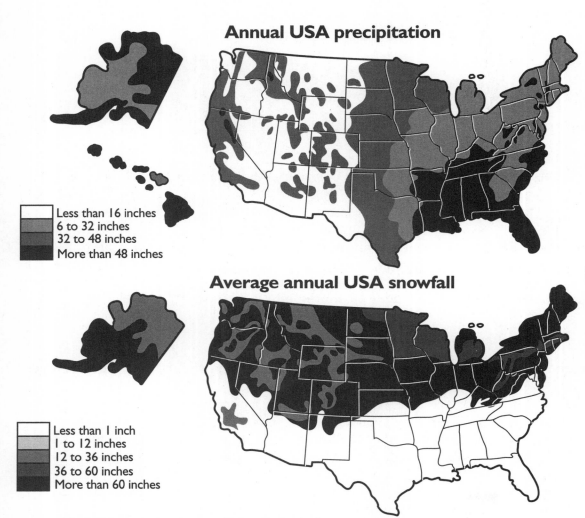

Annual USA precipitation

Less than 16 inches
6 to 32 inches
32 to 48 inches
More than 48 inches

Average annual USA snowfall

Less than 1 inch
1 to 12 inches
12 to 36 inches
36 to 60 inches
More than 60 inches

Average Annual Overall Precipitation

Precipitation (pree-SIP-uh-TAY-shun) is any kind of water that falls out of clouds—rain, snow, sleet, hail, or drizzle. Weather scientists keep track of the yearly—or annual—precipitation so they can compare it year after year. In the United States it's measured in inches of liquid water, or rain.

Average Annual Snowfall

Snowfall is one particular kind of precipitation. Its depth is measured in inches in the United States. But one inch of snow doesn't equal one inch of rain or overall precipitation. It takes about ten inches of snow to make one inch of rain.

48

Build a Weather Station: Rain Gauge

Cut out the scale. Tape it to the bottle. Make sure you attach the scale to the part of the bottle that is a uniform shape.

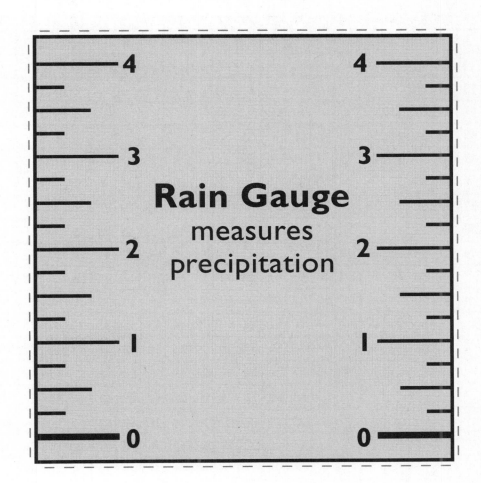

The Wow's and Why's of Weather Scholastic Professional Books

Build a Weather Station: Psychrometer

Make a copy of this page and keep it with your psychrometer (si-CHROM-uh-ter).
A psychrometer measures relative humidity.

Find the Relative Humidity

Dry-Bulb Temperatures (°F)

Wet-Bulb Temp (°F)	56	58	60	62	64	66	68	70	71	72	73	74	75	76	77	78	79	80	82	84	86	88
38	7	2																				
40	15	11	7																			
42	25	19	14	9	7																	
44	34	29	22	17	13	8	4															
46	45	38	30	24	18	14	10	6	4	3	1											
48	55	47	40	33	26	21	16	12	10	9	7	5	4	3	1							
50	66	56	48	41	34	29	23	19	17	15	13	11	9	8	6	5	4	3				
52	77	67	57	50	43	36	31	25	23	21	19	17	15	13	12	10	9	7	5	3	1	
54	88	76	68	59	51	44	38	33	30	28	25	23	21	19	17	16	14	12	10	7	5	3
56		89	79	66	60	53	46	40	37	34	32	29	27	25	23	21	19	18	14	12	9	7
58			89	79	70	61	54	48	45	42	39	36	34	31	29	27	25	23	20	18	14	11
60				90	79	71	62	55	52	48	46	43	40	38	35	33	31	29	25	21	18	15
62					90	80	71	64	60	57	53	50	47	44	42	39	37	35	30	28	23	20
64						90	80	72	68	65	61	58	54	51	48	46	43	41	36	32	28	25
66							90	81	77	73	69	65	62	59	58	53	50	47	42	37	33	30
68								90	86	82	78	74	70	66	63	60	57	54	48	43	39	35
70									95	91	88	82	78	74	71	67	64	61	55	49	44	40
72											95	91	88	82	79	75	71	68	61	56	50	46
74													96	91	87	83	79	75	69	62	57	51
76															96	91	87	83	76	69	63	57
78																	96	91	84	78	70	64
80																			82	84	77	70
82																				92	84	77
84																					92	85
86																						92

The Wow's and Why's of Weather Scholastic Professional Books

Wind

Why the Winds Blow

Wind is air on the move. Winds can vary from a gentle breeze to a hurricane gale, but all wind results from temperature differences in the atmosphere. Air receives its heat from the ocean or land beneath it. Because the sun unevenly heats the earth's surface—the equator gets more solar heating than the poles, for example—the air above the surface in turn receives varying amounts of heat depending on latitude, season, and geographical features such as mountains or oceans (see Chapter 2). Air above warm areas expands and rises, and cooler air flows in to replace it. That rising and flowing air is wind.

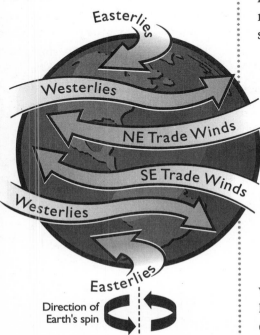

Direction of Earth's spin

Warm air rising over the equator and being replaced by cooler air from higher latitudes creates global, or prevailing, winds. These winds are responsible for the general circulation of the atmosphere. If Earth stood still, these winds would blow in a straight line. But the planet is spinning, so winds curve as they blow. This is called the Coriolis effect. The atmosphere's general circulation, along with the Coriolis effect, combine to produce the north and south polar easterly winds, the prevailing westerlies at the mid-latitudes, and the northeast and southwest trade winds on both sides of the equator (see diagram). The strongest westerlies occur at heights of 6-12 miles (10-20 km) and are concentrated in narrow channels of fast-moving upper atmospheric air called jet streams. Jet streams in both hemispheres usually follow the boundaries between cold and warm air and can exceed 200 mph (320 km per hour).

All winds are named for the direction from which they blow. The northeast trade winds in the Northern Hemisphere blow from the east toward the west, for example. The exact position of prevailing winds and jet streams change throughout the year and sometimes shift a bit from one year to the next, but they are major permanent forces in determining the climates of the planet.

Smaller-Scale Winds

Prevailing winds cause the general circulation of the earth's atmosphere; within that circulation are smaller-scale winds. Whereas prevailing winds play an important part in determining the climate of an area, smaller-scale winds drive its day-to-day weather. These synoptic-scale winds are air moving around small areas of high and low pressure in the atmosphere. Air flows toward a low-pressure area (low). Because of the Coriolis effect, that means that winds blow counterclockwise around a low. Alternately, air flows away from a high-pressure area (high). Therefore, winds blow clockwise around a high. In simple terms, this means that if you stand with your back to the wind in the Northern Hemisphere, a low-pressure area is at your left and a high-pressure area at your right.

Local winds are winds that blow only in a specific place. Sea or lake breezes between land and water are a common type of local wind. Land heats and cools faster than water, so warm air over land rises and cooler air over the ocean or a lake blows in to replace it during the day. The reverse can happen at night as the land cools faster than the water.

Storm Science: TORNADOES

Tornadoes are the most violent storms on the earth. Their funnel shape is a swirling vortex of spinning air. The largest tornadoes can have winds as fast as 300 mph (480 km)—the fastest winds on the planet's surface. Winds of this intensity can lift trains and trucks, smash houses, and make projectile missiles out of cars. Although tornadoes are intense storms that do millions of dollars of damage and kill dozens of people a year in North America, most are short-lived and confined to small areas. The average tornado lasts only a few minutes and forges paths under a mile long.

Thunderstorms spawn tornadoes. The biggest twisters come from supercell storms—giant, towering, cumulonimbus thunderstorms that soar toward the stratosphere and are often ten miles in diameter. It's no coincidence that Tornado Alley runs from Iowa to Texas. Springtime supercell storms form in this part of the United States as warm, moist air from the Gulf of Mexico moves north and begins to rise, encountering unstable air and winds of different speeds as it climbs and condenses into a towering thunderhead cloud. These variable winds in the growing thunderstorm set some of the air in the storm spinning horizontally. Updrafts in the storm tilt this tube of spinning air on its end, creating what's called a mesocyclone. A mesocyclone is a rotating column of air inside a thunderstorm and provides the vertical spin that tornadoes need. Just exactly how a piece of that vertical spin tightens, speeds up, and drops out of the cloud as a tornado isn't completely understood by scientists.

Fujita Tornado Scale

Fujita number	Wind speed mph	Observed Damage
F0	40-72	**Light:** Knocked-over chimneys and billboards, broken branches.
F1	73-112	**Moderate:** Roof and garage damage, mobile homes moved.
F2	113-157	**Significant:** Trees snapped, roofs torn off, boxcars overturned
F3	158-206	**Severe:** Trees uprooted, cars lifted and tossed, trains overturned.
F4	207-260	**Devastating:** Well-built homes leveled, cars become missiles.
F5	261-318	**Incredible:** Strong homes lifted off foundations and destroyed, steel-reinforced concrete structures badly damaged.

How a tornado is formed.

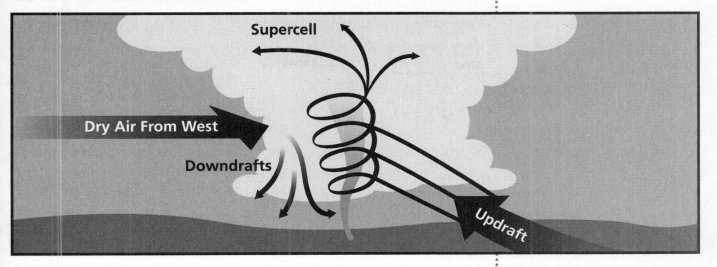

Supercell

Dry Air From West

Downdrafts

Updraft

Weather and the Environment

AIR POLLUTION AND THERMAL INVERSIONS

In general, temperature decreases as altitude increases—a mountain's top is colder than its valley. This pattern ensures mixing of the atmosphere because the low warm air rises, then cools as it reaches high altitudes and sinks, and is subsequently warmed and rises again. However, sometimes a layer of warm air stalls over a layer of cooler air and traps it. This is called a thermal inversion. The cooler air close to the ground is trapped because it is heavier than the warm air above it, and heavier air sinks. Inversions are common and many dissipate quickly. But inversions that stick around greatly aggravate the buildup of air pollution from factories, cars, power plants, and trucks. An inversion keeps the polluted air down near the surface, preventing winds from mixing it into the atmosphere where it can be diluted.

What atmospheric conditions can produce inversions? Stationary high-pressure systems with low winds can cause an inversion at the surface. But sometimes they are caused simply by nighttime surface cooling in an area. These nighttime inversions are usually dispersed by the next morning's midday sun. Geographical features, such as the semi-permanent high-pressure system off of the Southern California coast, are another cause of inversions. And in colder climates and in the winter, inversions are more common when the surface loses more heat than it gains.

Within days, the atmospheric mixing halted by an inversion can lead to hazardous concentrations of pollutants. An inversion over Donora, Pennsylvania, in 1948 led to the deaths of 20 people and respiratory illness in thousands. The severity of the chemical spill disaster at Bhopal, India, in 1984 that killed at least 3,300 people was due in part to a thermal inversion that concentrated the lethal chemical near the earth's surface.

Tornado Chaser
HOWARD BLUESTEIN

[ONLINE]
LINK

Kids' Tornado Page
http://whyfiles.news.
wisc.edu/013tornado

Find out what's got
Bluestein so fascinated
on this information-
packed site.

Most people run away from tornadoes. Not Howard Bluestein. He chases them!

Bluestein is a university professor and research meteorologist who studies tornadoes and how they form. Why doesn't he study the storms from a safe distance? "Tornadoes are very difficult to study because it's so hard to make measurements," explains Bluestein. "They don't last long, they encompass a small area, and they're difficult to predict."

Bluestein and his storm chasing graduate students at the University of Oklahoma spend April through June driving thousands of miles around Oklahoma, Texas, and Kansas, chasing down tornadoes. "It would be fascinating to actually get inside the tornado and take a look around," says Bluestein. "Since we can't, we try to get close enough to aim our portable radar unit and measure the wind field in and around the tornado. That information helps us to learn more about how twisters form."

Tornadoes and other severe weather have fascinated this storm chaser since a twister hit near his home in Massachusetts when he was a small boy. He was also interested in astronomy and electronics and at 12 years of age became a licensed amateur radio operator—something many storm watchers have in common. As a college student, Bluestein studied electrical engineering, but credits an inspiring professor with his conversion to meteorology. He's been studying tornadoes ever since and figures that over the past 20 years he's seen more than one hundred. One especially fierce twister Bluestein was chasing in April of 1991 had winds of 280 mph (448 km). It was the first F5 tornado to have its winds officially recorded (not estimated). It also came a little too close for comfort. "The tornado leaped across the road right in front of us," recalls Bluestein. "You could see its furious spin. It was very, very clear." *Photo courtesy of Howard Bluestein*

Reading the Wind

I n 1805 a British naval admiral named Sir Francis Beaufort invented a wind-measuring scale based on observations of waves and ship sails. Wind strengths were divided into 13 categories called forces. This Beaufort scale was later adapted for land use and is still used today to estimate wind speeds. In this activity students use their powers of observation to estimate wind speed, comparing what they see to the Beaufort scale.

Materials
(for class)

reproducible page 61

A Week of Wind	Monday
by	What's the wind like today?
(your name)	
Tuesday	Beaufort scale number
What's the wind like today?	Wednesday
	What's the wind like today?
Beaufort scale number	Beaufort scale number
Thursday	Friday
What's the wind like today?	What's the wind like today?
Beaufort scale number	Beaufort scale number

Directions

Reproduce page 61 and distribute it to students. Ask them to read though the descriptions of wind effects. Invite students to create a chart like the one shown that they can use to record the wind, in Beaufort units, in the morning and afternoon, for a week or so.

Feeling the Chill

W ind can make cold temperatures feel even colder. That's because the wind blows away the normal layer of warmed air covering human skin. The heat escapes, and you feel colder. The faster the wind, the faster the heat is carried away, and the colder it feels. This is called the windchill index or factor. It's a temperature that represents how cold it feels. Students can discover the chilling difference wind makes in this activity.

Materials
(for class)

reproducible page 62

Answers: 1. 40°F
2. -15°F 3. 20 mph
4. 20°F 5. 35 mph
6. 30°F

Directions

Make copies of page 62 and hand out one to each student. Show students how to read the table. The actual air temperature runs across the top, and the wind speed on the left. The windchill temperature is found by intersecting the two. Ask students to use the table to answer the questions.

Build a Weather Station

ANEMOMETER

Students can measure wind speed by making and using this pressure-type anemometer. Note: This anemometer will give general indications of wind speed, not precise measurements. Follow the suggestions and guidelines carefully to obtain the most accurate readings.

Materials

(for each group)

reproducible page 63

cardboard

table tennis ball

brightly colored heavy thread or thin string

tape

glue

scissors

paper clip

Instrument of Interest: **The Anemometer**

An anemometer (an-uh-MOM-uh-ter) is an instrument designed to measure wind speed. The earliest wind-speed indicator was probably the pressure anemometer. It featured a hanging plate along a curved scale. As the wind strength increased, it forced the plate higher along the scale. The most commonly used anemometers in weather stations today are rotation anemometers. These instruments consist of three or four conical cups attached to short rods that are connected at right angles to a vertical shaft. As the wind blows, the cups are pushed, which turns the shaft. The number of turns per minute is usually translated into wind speed by a system of gears leading to a readout.

Directions

Divide the class into small groups. Make a copy of the anemometer pattern on page 63 for each group and have students follow these instructions:

1 Cut out the anemometer pattern on page 63 and glue it to cardboard. Let it dry and cut it out.

2 Unbend a paper clip and use it to poke a hole where the black dot appears on the top of the scale.

3 Thread a 12-inch piece of thread through the hole and tape it to the back.

4 Tape the table tennis ball to the other end of the thread. It's done!

5 To use the anemometer, face into the wind (the direction of the arrow) and hold the instrument so the top line is level. The wind lifts the table tennis ball, moving the thread along the wind speed scale. The thread's height along the scale indicates the speed. The ball should move in a smooth upward lift. If it's moving away from the anemometer, move to stand more directly into the wind. (Students can make a chart and record the winds twice a day, then compare their readings with their Beaufort scale observations (page 61).)

Look at this line to keep it level.

HOLD HERE!

CUT OUT

39

34

29

25

21

17

14

11

8

MPH

Anomometer (an-uh-MOM-uh-ter) measures wind speed

Build a Weather Station

WIND VANE

Knowing the wind direction is an essential element in weather forecasting. The wind vane, or weather vane, is probably the oldest of all meteorological instruments. This activity allows students to make a wind vane and track the direction of winds over time.

Directions

Divide the class into small groups and make one copy of page 64 for each group. Have students follow these instructions:

1 Cut out the two patterns on the page.

2 Use the wind pointer pattern to cut a pointer out of heavy cardboard or plastic foam. Glue the direction disk onto cardboard or plastic foam. (You can waterproof cardboard pieces by covering them with laminating film; the direction disk can be covered with plastic wrap.) Poke a hole in the center of the disk where the dot is. It needs to be big enough for a pencil to fit through.

3 Push the pencil, eraser-side down, through the hole in the direction disk. Stick the eraser end into a small ball of clay and set it in the bottom of a can and fill with sand or gravel. This will make it stable.

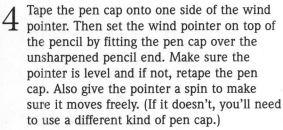

4 Tape the pen cap onto one side of the wind pointer. Then set the wind pointer on top of the pencil by fitting the pen cap over the unsharpened pencil end. Make sure the pointer is level and if not, retape the pen cap. Also give the pointer a spin to make sure it moves freely. (If it doesn't, you'll need to use a different kind of pen cap.)

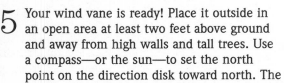

5 Your wind vane is ready! Place it outside in an open area at least two feet above ground and away from high walls and tall trees. Use a compass—or the sun—to set the north point on the direction disk toward north. The wind pointer's narrow end will swing into the wind, indicating the direction the wind is coming *from.* If the pointer is pointing to the west, the wind is blowing from the west and is called a westerly wind.

6 Check the wind direction using the wind vanes twice daily and record the direction on a chart.

Extension
Weather and wind vanes have traditionally been decorative as well as functional. Invite students to decorate their wind pointers and direction disks.

Materials
(for each group)

reproducible page 64

heavy cardboard or plastic foam meat tray or egg carton lid

unsharpened pencil

pen cap that fits loosely over pencil end

scissors

heavy waterproof tape

compass (optional)

glue

empty coffee can

sand or fine gravel

modeling clay

clear contact paper or laminating film (optional)

The Power of Wind

Wind is moving air, and moving air has the power to move things! Sailboats, windmills, and kites are all examples of things that move thanks to the power of wind. In this activity students assemble pinwheels and then use them to measure the lifting power of their own wind source—their breath.

Materials

(for each student)

reproducible page 65

scissors

pushpin

unsharpened pencil

small paper cup

tape

heavy thread

small uniform objects such as coins, marbles, erasers, paper clips, etc.

Directions

Make one copy of reproducible page 65 for each student. Then have students follow these instructions:

1 Cut out the pinwheel pattern along the dashed lines. Set aside the data sheet.

2 Hold the pinwheel pattern up to the light or against a window and trace the middle dot onto the back.

3 Set the pattern face down on a notebook. Carefully bend—but don't crease—the pinwheel "arms" inward one at a time until all the dots are piled on top of each other over the center dot. Then push the pushpin through the center.

4 Attach the assembled pinwheel onto the end of a pencil by pushing the pushpin into the end of the eraser as far as it will go.

5 Tape one end of a 12-inch piece of heavy thread to the middle of the pencil and the other end to the outside of a paper cup.

6 Loosely hold the pencil between your index and middle fingers and blow on the pinwheel to make it spin. Practice this for awhile, noticing how the thread wraps around the pencil. (Is the pinwheel spinning but the pencil isn't turning? Push the pushpin farther into the eraser.)

7 Experiment lifting different small objects in the cup and record your findings on the data sheet.

Note: Make sure students understand that each try is a single breath (gust of wind) and that they'll be calculating an average after performing the three tries. Challenge students to infer and rank the comparative weight of their tested objects based on the number of string wraps: What was heaviest? lightest?

Twister Totals

Storm Science: TORNADOES

Tornadoes are rare in Washington, but all too common in Kansas. Colorado has a lot of small tornadoes, but very few strong ones. Challenge students to find out other fascinating tornado facts by reading the map on page 66.

Directions

Reproduce page 66 and distribute it to students. Review the information on the map with students before having them answer the questions on their own. Ensure that students understand that the first number is the total number of tornadoes that occurred in 1995 and the second number is how many "significant" tornadoes occurred during that year—tornadoes that rated between F2 and F5 on the Fujita scale. This activity is a great opportunity to review state abbreviations as well.

Extension

Have students investigate the difference between a tornado watch and a tornado warning. What is the safety protocol for such severe weather occurrences at their school?

Book Break

The Night of the Twisters by Ivy Ruckman (HarperTrophy, 1986)

After they read this contemporary classic, challenge students to retell the story in the book as a news article or TV news bulletin.

Materials
(for the class)

reproducible page 66

Answers: 1. Washington, Alaska, Hawaii, Maine, Rhode Island, and Vermont 2. Texas 3. Texas 4. Four—TX, KY, KS, IA 5. Kentucky. 14 of its 30 tornadoes were F2s or higher—47% Bonus: Mostly central and southern states

The Federal Emergency Management Agency's Site for Kids http://www.fema.gov/ kids

Students can visit this link to play games and take quizzes about tornadoes and other storms; share stories, poems, and artwork about surviving natural disasters; and write to kids who have been through disasters.

Inverting Air

Weather and the Environment:
AIR POLLUTION AND THERMAL INVERSIONS

Thermal inversions can greatly increase pollution by trapping pollutants near the surface and preventing the pollutants from mixing and diluting in the atmosphere. In this demonstration students can see how warm air traps cold air beneath it.

Materials
(for the whole class)

two identical glass jars

incense

two pieces of paperboard, thin cardboard, or posterboard

black paper

lamp

grease pencil, permanent marker, or crayon

Directions

1. Set a lamp near a dark background, such as black paper taped over a stack of books.

2. Set one of the glass jars upside down and write *WARM* on it. Set the other jar rightside up and write *COLD* on it.

3. Fill the COLD jar with smoke by holding it upside down over burning incense. Quickly cover the jar with a piece of cardboard.

4. Cool the air in the jar. Either set the jar in a freezer or in a bowl of ice. Be careful not to let out the smoke!

5. Heat the air in the WARM jar. You can set the jar on a radiator or in an oven for a few minutes. Or pour hot water into the jar, dump it out, and dry it thoroughly. (Optional: Placing a piece of cardboard over the jar will help trap the warm air inside the jar.)

6. Take the COLD jar out of the freezer and set it in front of the dark background so the smoke is clearly visible. Then turn the WARM jar upside down and set it directly on top of the COLD jar. Immediately slide out the cardboard. Ask: *What happens?* (Nothing; the cold smoky air stays in the bottom jar.) *Why?* (Cold air is heavier than warm air; it sinks and stays on the bottom.) *How is this like an inversion that aggravates air pollution?* (The upper warm air traps cooler polluted air at the surface where it can't escape.)

7. Carefully invert both jars so the warm air is at the bottom and the cold air at the top. Ask: *What happens?* (The smoke first blows—like wind—into the bottom jar and then the smoke becomes evenly distributed in both jars.) *Why?* (Hot air rises from the bottom jar and the cold, smoky air is sucked down to replace it, and the air mixes.)

Extension

This activity will allow students to discover the amount of particulate air pollution around them. Have students stick loops of light-colored masking tape (or strips of double-sided tape) onto index cards so each one has a square of sticky surface. Invite students to attach their cards to different structures inside and outside, with the taped area exposed. After a few days have students retrieve the cards and observe what particles they've collected with magnifying lenses. How do the cards left in different places compare?

Name_____

The Beaufort Wind Scale

Beaufort Number	Kind of Wind	Wind Speed	Effects of Wind
0	Calm	less than 1 mph	Air feels still. Smoke rises straight up. Weather or wind vane doesn't move.
1	Light air	1-3 mph	Smoke drifts a little as it rises. Weather vane doesn't move.
2	Slight Breeze	4-7 mph	Can feel wind on face. Smoke follows wind. Leaves rustle. Flags stir. Weather vanes move.
3	Gentle Breeze	8-12 mph	Leaves and twigs move constantly. Light flags extend.
4	Moderate Breeze	13-18 mph	Dust, loose paper, and leaves blow about. Thin tree branches sway. Flags flap.
5	Fresh Breeze	19-24 mph	Small trees sway. Small waves crest on lakes and streams. Flags ripple.
6	Strong Breeze	25-31 mph	Thick tree branches sway constantly. Flags beat. Umbrellas turn inside out.
7	Moderate Gale	32-38 mph	Big trees sway. The wind pushes when walking against it. Flags extend completely.
8	Fresh Gale	39-46 mph	Twigs are torn off trees. Walking against wind is difficult.
9	Strong Gale	47-54 mph	Slight building damage–antennas and shingles blow off and awnings rip. Tree branches break.
10	Whole Gale	55-63 mph	Trees snap or are uprooted. Buildings are damaged.
11	Storm	64-73 mph	Widespread building damage. Cars overturn, trees uproot or snap and blow away.
12	Hurricane	74+ mph	Violent destruction and widespread damage. Buildings are destroyed.

The Wow's and Why's of Weather Scholastic Professional Books

The Wind's Chill

Ever notice how the wind makes you *feel* colder? That extra coldness is called the windchill factor. The wind whisks away the layer of warm air that covers your skin—so you feel colder. Use this windchill factor table to answer the questions.

Wind Speed (mph)	Actual Thermometer Readings (°F)									
	50	**40**	**30**	**20**	**10**	**0**	**-10**	**-20**	**-30**	**-40**
	Wind Chill Temperatures (°F)									
0	50	40	30	20	10	0	-10	-20	-30	-40
5	48	37	27	16	6	-5	-15	-26	-36	-47
10	40	28	16	4	-9	-21	-33	-46	-58	-70
15	36	22	9	-5	-18	-36	-45	-58	-72	-85
20	32	18	4	-10	-25	-39	-53	-67	-82	-96
25	30	16	0	-15	-29	-44	-59	-74	-88	-104
30	28	13	-2	-18	-33	-48	-63	-79	-94	-109
35	27	11	-4	-20	-35	-49	-67	-82	-98	-113
40	26	10	-6	-21	-37	-53	-69	-85	-100	-116

Questions

1 It's 50°F outside, and the winds are blowing at 10 mph. How cold does it feel? _____

2 The winds are blowing at a mild 5 mph today. But it's -10°F! How cold does it feel?

_____

3 The windchill temperature feels like -10°F even though the actual air temperature is 20°F.

How fast must the wind be blowing? _____

4 It's a windy day. The winds are blowing at 25 mph. The temperature feels like -15°F.

What is the actual air temperature? _____

5 It's 0°F outside. What wind speed will make it feel like -49°F?

_____

6 If the winds are calm and the temperature is 30°F, how cold does it feel?

_____

The Wow's and Why's of Weather Scholastic Professional Books

Build a Weather Station: Anemometer

Cut out the anemometer pattern to make your own instrument to measure wind speed.

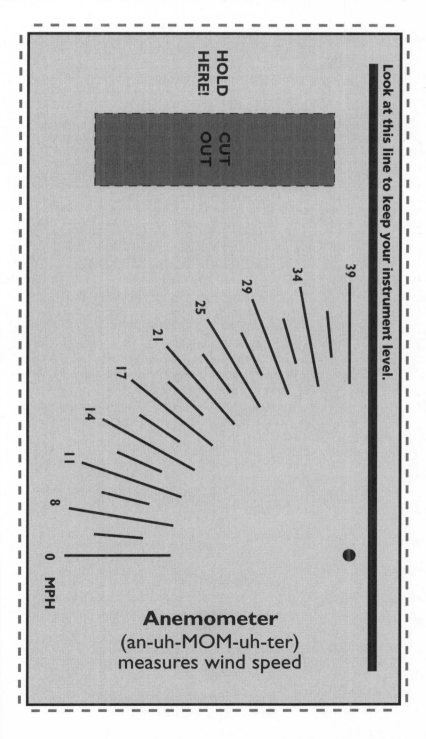

HOLD HERE!

CUT OUT

Look at this line to keep your instrument level.

39
34
29
25
21
17
14
11
8
0
MPH

Anemometer
(an-uh-MOM-uh-ter)
measures wind speed

Build a Weather Station: Wind Vane

Cut out the patterns on this page to make a wind vane.

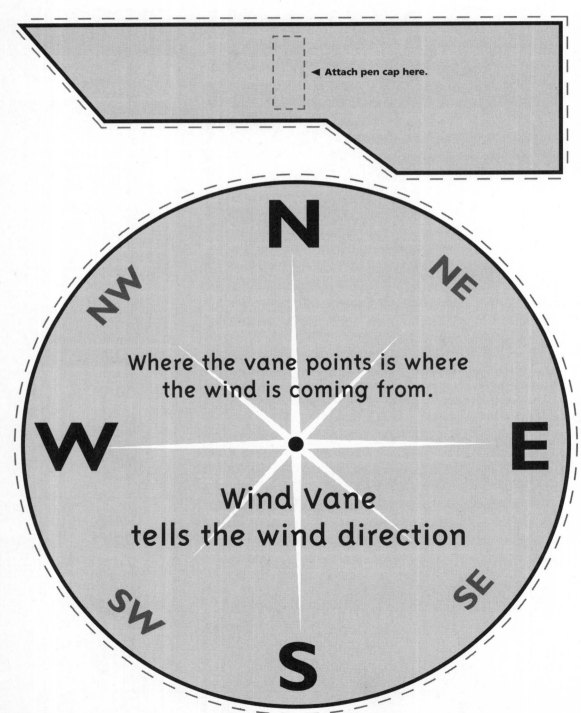

◄ Attach pen cap here.

N

NE

NW

Where the vane points is where the wind is coming from.

W

E

Wind Vane
tells the wind direction

SW

SE

S

The Wow's and Why's of Weather Scholastic Professional Books

Name _____

The Power of Wind

Cut out the pinwheel pattern and the data sheet.

Name _____

Pinwheel Power Data Sheet Number of String Wraps

What's in the cup?	1st try	2nd try	3rd try	Total (Add 1st, 2nd, & 3rd)	Average (divide total by 3)
Nothing					

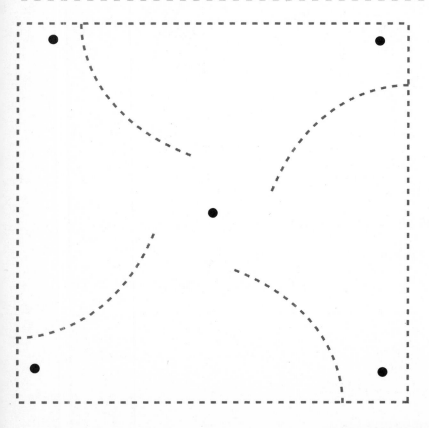

The Wow's and Why's of Weather Scholastic Professional Books

Twister Totals

Tornadoes come in six strengths. They are ranked F0-F5 on what's called the Fujita scale. An F5 tornado is the strongest. It has winds of at least 261 mph (tk km)!

The map below shows all 1,233 tornadoes reported for 1995. The first number in each state is the total number of tornadoes that year. The second number is the number of significant twisters--tornadoes that rated F2-F5. Use the map to answer the questions.

Questions

1 What six states had absolutely no tornadoes in 1995?_____

2 What state had the most total tornadoes?_____

3 What state had the most "significant" (F2-F5) tornadoes?_____

4 How many states had ten or more significant tornadoes?_____

5 What state had the highest percentage of significant tornadoes compared to total tornadoes?

_____

Bonus:

Use a pencil to shade in the states with 25 or more total tornadoes. In what parts of the country are most of these states?_____

The Wow's and Why's of Weather Scholastic Professional Books

Weather Watching and Forecasting

On the Lookout for Weather

Humans have a great interest in watching and predicting the weather. Weather not only influences what we'll wear or whether we'll go on a picnic. It can also make or break a harvest, bring about a heating fuel shortage, or—in the case of severe storms—cause widespread destruction and even death.

People have been observing and tracking wind, rain, cloud, and temperature patterns throughout history in an attempt to predict the weather to come. All cultures are filled with weather folklore and sayings such as, "Red sky at night, sailors delight. Red sky at morning, sailors take warning" that are a testament to humankind's interest in weather watching and forecasting. Even in modern times, people still use simple instruments, some basic knowledge, and keen observations to predict unfolding local weather conditions for themselves.

High-Tech Weather Watchers

Scientists with the job of forecasting detailed weather conditions for large regions over many days need a sophisticated array of high-tech equipment. Weather stations measure and record the same weather conditions discussed in this book—namely temperature, barometric pressure, humidity, wind speed, and wind direction. These weather stations, however, use more sophisticated instruments to record local ground-level conditions and transmit them from thousands of positions to central forecasting offices. Aircraft collect information about upper-level winds, while ships and buoys provide data about the weather above oceans. Weather balloons measure temperature, humidity, and pressure at different heights, providing a vertical profile of weather conditions. Helium-filled weather balloons carry instruments that collect and transmit weather data (called radiosondes) until they reach a height where they burst and parachute back to the ground.

Satellites are another important weather-gathering tool. Their images of the globe allow scientists to see clouds from above and to spot storms and hurricanes developing over the oceans. Satellites also provide temperatures of cloud tops, the upper atmosphere, and the oceans, as well as wind speeds and the location of otherwise invisible water vapor.

Radar is used to show where rain, snow, hail, or other precipitation is falling—and how heavy it is. Radar works by sending out radio waves and analyzing their returning echoes to infer what they bounced off. Doppler radar is a new and improved type of radar that not only measures precipitation but shows wind speed and direction, which meteorologists can use to interpret the boundaries between warm and cool air (fronts).

Mapping Out a Forecast

Much of the improvement in weather forecasting over the past 30 years is thanks to number-crunching computers. Without them, forecasts of more than a few hours would be impossible. Weather data is gathered from satellites, stations, radar, etc. The data—including temperature, pressure, wind, and humidity—are fed into a computer that makes a grid covering the whole planet from the sea into the stratosphere. The computer uses mathematical equations to project how the conditions will change over time and churn out forecasts. The current data is also displayed in what's called a synoptic chart, or weather map. Professional weather maps often use cryptic symbols, but simplified weather maps appear in nearly every newspaper and help the public understand the weather.

Even with radar, satellites, and supercomputers, weather forecasting has its limits. The National Weather Service issues short-range forecasts and extended forecasts. Short-range forecasts predict the weather over the next 18-36 hours and are considered to forecast general conditions such as temperature and precipitation with good accuracy. Extended forecasts usually predict the weather over the next five days and are much less reliable. Daily temperature forecasts for three to five days ahead are more likely to be accurate than predictions of precipitation because the conditions that determine precipitation are more variable. Even with inevitable improvements in weather-collecting instruments and more understanding of atmospheric phenomena, many scientists doubt that accurate weather forecasts of more than two weeks ahead will ever be possible. The weather is dependent on too many interrelated and unpredictable factors.

Storm Science: WINTER STORMS

Winter storms bring some of the worst weather around—snow, sleet, freezing rain, fierce winds, and plunging temperatures. The heaviest snowfalls often occur when the air temperature is hovering around freezing. If the snow falls through air that changes temperature a few degrees one way or the other, it could end up as rain, sleet, or freezing rain (see diagram). A mixture of different kinds of precipitation is in fact very likely because the storms that bring snow are often caused by warm fronts sliding over cold air near the ground.

A notorious example of a winter storm is a northeaster, a late fall or winter storm along the Atlantic Coast of North America that brings heavy rain, heavy snow, and severe coastal flooding. The storm is named for the strong northeast winds they produce.

Any winter storm becomes a blizzard if snow is falling, winds are faster than 35 mph (56 km per hour), and visibility is one-quarter mile (.4 km) or less. Under these conditions the National Weather Service issues a blizzard warning.

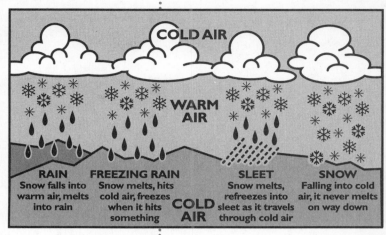

COLD AIR

WARM AIR

RAIN Snow falls into warm air, melts into rain

FREEZING RAIN Snow melts, hits cold air, freezes when it hits something

COLD AIR

SLEET Snow melts, refreezes into sleet as it travels through cold air

SNOW Falling into cold air, it never melts on way down

Weather and the Environment

EL NIÑO

El Niño is an abnormal warming of the tropical Pacific Ocean that can alter weather around the globe. It's part of the El Niño Southern Oscillation (ENSO), a cycle of changing ocean temperatures, rainfall, atmospheric circulation, vertical motion, and air pressure over the tropical Pacific. An El Niño episode is a warming of the tropical Pacific Ocean, while a cooling is called a La Niña. An El Niño happens every 3 to 4 years on average and each lasts 12 to 18 months. Sometimes a cooling La Niña follows an El Niño—but not always.

What causes an El Niño? A dying down of the trade winds that normally push the top layer of sun-soaked warm ocean water over to the west side of the Pacific Ocean. During an El Niño this Pacific Ocean pattern of hot on the west side and cool on the east side breaks down. The trade winds slack off, and the warm water sloshes away from the west side spreading east. "Instead of being warmest in the western equatorial Pacific, it becomes uniformly warmer across the entire basin," explains Vernon Kousky, National Oceanic and Atmospheric Administration's (NOAA) meteorologist. Thunderstorms start to form over the warm shifting water, and entire weather patterns in the Pacific are changed as a result.

The ENSO cycle is a natural part of the planet's climate system. It's a way excess heat in the tropics is exported. (Hurricanes are another smaller way.) But although its natural, an El Niño creates ocean and weather conditions that are not normal. This means floods, droughts, and storms that take a toll on the environment.

TV Weather Forecaster

GARY AMBLE

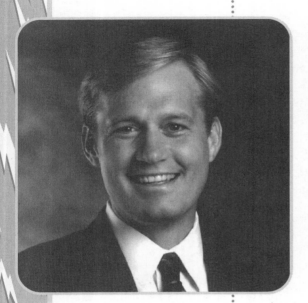

Gary Amble puts his reputation on the line every night at 5, 6, and 10 o'clock. He's the Chief Meteorologist at KCTV Channel 5 in Kansas City. Every night he reports the weather—good or bad—and gives a forecast of what's to come. "I think the vast majority of people realize that you're just the messenger," says Amble. But some people do seem to hold him personally responsible for the weather at times—and the weddings or picnics it has ruined. It's all part of being a TV personality.

But TV weather forecasters aren't just pretty faces. Most—like Amble—are trained meteorologists recognized by the American Meteorological Society (AMS). They need at least a bachelor's degree that includes 20 semester hours of meteorology. "To get your AMS seal, [the Society] requires your consecutive weathercasts to be judged by some of your top peers within the Society," explains Amble.

Gary Amble's road to the world of weather began in college, where he studied science. He also got television experience at a small cable station in his college town. That was important, because TV weather forecasters need to be comfortable working on live television. Most forecasters on TV stand in front of what looks like a weather map, but it's actually just a blank wall. They only know where to point by looking at TV screens off camera—kind of like gesturing in a mirror. It can make for confusion. "Unexpected things happen almost every single night," says Amble.

Gathering weather information and making accurate forecasts is just part of television weather forecasters' jobs these days. Most also visit local schools and scout groups, teaching kids about the science behind what they see in the sky and on the TV weather map.

Photo courtesy of Gary Amble and KCTV

Mapping It Out

Weather maps in newspapers and on TV have become a common sight and are now part of how the public interprets weather information. Highs, lows, and fronts have become a part of our vocabulary. In these two activities students will become familiar with some common weather map symbols and use them to first read, and then create, a weather map.

Directions

1 Photocopy and hand out page 77 to students. Go over the symbols for precipitation, pressure areas, and fronts along the bottom of the page, checking that students understand their meanings. Note: Showers mean intermittent precipitation that can be either light or heavy. Cold fronts are often colored blue, warm fronts red, and stationary fronts alternate red and blue in colored weather maps. Consider inviting students to color the fronts on the key and the map accordingly.

2 Spend some time talking about the ways temperature is displayed on the map. Specific cities have forecasted high/low temperatures. Ask: *Have these temperatures occurred?* (No, they're forecasted temperatures.) *Are they in degrees Celsius or Fahrenheit?* (Fahrenheit)

3 Lines dividing areas of equal temperature, called isotherms, also traverse the map. (Also in degrees Fahrenheit.) The isotherm temperatures are in small circles along or at the ends of the lines. Many colored weather maps these days—such as those in *USA Today*—color-code their isotherms for easier reading. Invite students to do so on their maps by choosing a color for each temperature on the key along the bottom and then filling in the corresponding areas of the map.

4 Once students understand the map's components, allow them to answer the questions. Note: Supply a map of the U.S. to use as a reference by those students who can't identify the states on the map.

5 Photocopy and hand out page 78 to students. (They'll still need page 77 as a reference for symbols.)

6 Ask students to use the weather information below the blank map to draw in precipitation, fronts, and areas of high and low pressure.

Extension

Have student groups collect two week's worth of weather maps from a single source (a local or national newspaper or weather web site). Ask students to order the maps chronologically and compare them. Ask: *Which way do weather systems move? How long do fronts and high- and low- pressure systems last? What geographical features (latitude, mountain ranges, sea coast) affect temperatures?*

Materials
(for each student)

reproducible pages 77 and 78

colored pencils or crayons

reference map of the United States with states labeled (optional)

Answers to page 77:
1. Eastern 2. 38°F; Houston, Texas 3. stationary front 4. over Illinois 5. flurries, snow

Answer to page 78:

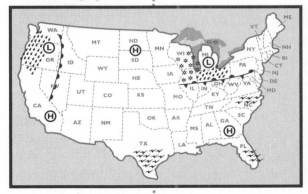

Build a Weather Station

CLASSROOM WEATHER STATION

Put it all together! Set up the weather instruments created throughout the book in one place in the classroom to make a weather station. Allow students the opportunity to record and track the changes in weather over a week—or longer.

Materials
(for the whole class)

rain gauge (page 41)

barometer (page 14)

thermometer (page 26)

anemometer (page 56)

wind vane (page 57)

psychrometer (page 42)

cloud key (page 39)

reproducible page 79

Directions

1 Set up the rain gauge, thermometer, and wind vane outside. (Note: Consider taking the thermometer and wind vane out in the morning and bringing them back in every afternoon—they'll hold up better that way. Remember that the rain gauge must be reset to 0 each day.) Set up the barometer inside.

2 Divide the class into five groups and make a copy of page 79 for each group. Assign each group a day of the school week.

3 Have the members of the first day's group take readings from outside, as well as use the cloud key and wind gauge to complete the readings on page 79, once in the morning and once in the afternoon. Allow students to post their reports on a designated section of bulletin board or wall.

4 Continue step 3 with the other groups throughout the week. At the end of the week, make a chart that combines all of the readings and ask students to draw conclusions about the week's weather. Consider comparing it to "real" weather reports from the week's newspapers.

Weather Instruments for Your Weather Center:

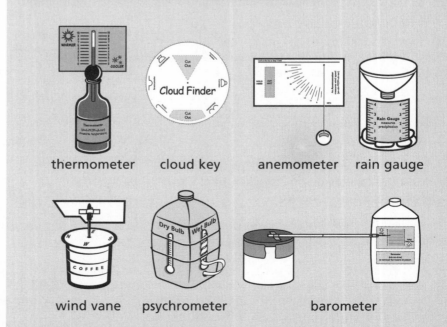

thermometer   cloud key   anemometer   rain gauge

wind vane   psychrometer   barometer

ACTIVITY

Winter Warnings

Storm Science: WINTER STORMS

Winter storms are indirect killers. People die not so much from the snow itself, as from the situations it creates. Traffic accidents caused by poor visibility and road conditions, hypothermia caused by low temperatures and windchill factors, and heart attacks caused by snow shoveling are the reason for most winter weather deaths. Fortunately, many of the hazards of winter storms can be avoided by being prepared and exercising caution. The National Weather Service (NWS) issues winter warnings, watches, and advisories to assist the public in preparing for and dealing with winter weather.

Directions

Assign student groups one of the five advisories listed below: blizzard warning, winter storm warning, winter storm watch, winter weather advisory, and frost/freeze warning. Challenge each group to investigate their advisory. What does it mean? When is it issued? What are its recommendations? (The National Weather Service, Federal Emergency Management Agency, and the Red Cross are all excellent sources.) Then have each group create an informational poster that (1) explains the meaning of the advisory, watch, or warning; (2) makes precautionary recommendations, and (3) makes suggestions for being prepared.

Winter Weather Advisories

- A **blizzard warning** advises people in the area to seek refuge and stay off the roads. Blinding snow, deep drifts, and life-threatening temperatures are probable.
- A **winter storm warning** is issued for heavy snow and ice and recommends staying indoors.
- A **winter storm watch** means the conditions exist for the possibility of heavy snow and possible ice and instructs people in the area to prepare now for the storm.
- A **winter weather advisory** indicates that weather conditions could make transportation difficult, but usually not life-threatening.
- A **frost/freeze warning** means that below freezing temperatures are expected and may cause damage to plants. People without heat are advised to seek shelter.

How to prepare for a Winter Storm

Things to have:
- a battery-powered radio
- extra food
- rock salt to melt ice
- flashlights
- wood for your fireplace

Water Warm-Up

Weather and the Environment: EL NIÑO

Materials

(for each group)

two identical clear jars (glass or plastic)

two pieces of heavy-duty aluminum foil (large enough to cover the mouth of the jars)

two ice cubes

two rubber bands

hot and cold water

grease pencil, permanent marker, or crayon

During an El Niño event, warm ocean water moves eastward. Along with the warm water goes precipitation, so the eastern Pacific gets too much rain while the western is left in drought. Warm water creates more precipitation than cold water because it evaporates more easily. Evaporated water—water vapor—in the air is what condenses into clouds that later generate rain. This activity allows students to investigate the connection between water temperature, cloud formation, and rain.

Directions

Divide the class into small groups or pairs. Then have them follow these instructions:

1 Use a grease pencil, permanent marker, or crayon to label one jar "hot" and the other "cold."

2 Fill the hot jar with hot tap water halfway, and the cold jar to an equal level with cold water.

3 Cover each jar with one of the pieces of foil. It should be stretched taut. Attach each piece with a rubber band.

4 Simultaneously place an ice cube on top of each jar. Wait about 10 minutes. You need to see "fog" in one of the jars before proceeding to step 5.

5 Remove the ice cubes. Then carefully turn over the pieces of foil and compare what you see. *What's on the inside of the foil?* (drops of water) *Where did it come from?* (It condensed from water vapor in the air inside the jar.) *What is this condensed water vapor like?* (cloud droplets) *Which jar produced more "clouds"?* (the hot water jar) *Why?* (Warm water evaporates more easily.)

Fact or Folklore?

Folklore around the world is full of sayings about and references to the weather. In this fun activity students assess the weather sense of six weather sayings.

Directions

Materials
(for each student)

reproducible page 80

1 Introduce the activity by asking students if anyone has heard the saying, "Red sky at night, sailors' delight. Red sky at morning, sailors take warning." Ask: *What does it mean?* (A red sunset brings dry weather, but a red sunrise brings rain.) Then discuss why the saying may or may not be true. Fiery red sunsets and sunrises are caused when light reflects off particles in the air—such as dust or cloud droplets. An extra-red sunset can mean that thin fair-weather cirrus clouds are in the west where most weather is coming from, so good weather is on the way. However, a red sunrise may mean the cirrus clouds in the east are on their way out—and storm clouds may be on the way in. So this is one example of a saying that is basically sound—except for the fact that dust and pollution can also cause a red sky. In those instances, the saying is *not* true.

2 Go over any vocabulary in the sayings that students may not be familiar with (such as "roosting," "descends," and "halo").

3 Now invite students to circle True or False for each of the six sayings on their papers and fill in the Why? or Why not? Encourage students to take a best guess based on what they have learned about weather so far.

4 Consider allowing students to form small groups to share and debate their choices before going over the answers.

Answers: 1. TRUE. Birds roost more during times of low air pressure—such as the time before a storm. Flying can be more difficult in lower pressure air with fewer updrafts. 2. FALSE. There's no evidence to support this claim, nor the same about woolly caterpillars. 3. TRUE. Unstable and humid air before a storm keeps smoke from chimneys and fires from rising quickly. 4. TRUE. A ring or halo around the moon is caused by light refracting (bending) in ice crystals in high-level clouds that often arrive ahead of a low-pressure storm system. 5. FALSE. A sunny day in February, which would allow a groundhog to see its shadow, has nothing to do with how long winter weather will last. 6. TRUE. There is more humidity in the air before it rains; it's soaked up by the moss, making it wet.

Extension

Invite students to write weather lore based on their own observations. Help them get started by asking brainstorming questions such as: *What does the sky look like before it snows or storms, or before a tornado? What does your dog do when it hears thunder?* They'll be surprised by the weather lore they already know!

Investigate a Weather Career

SCIENCE CAREERS

There are a number of individuals with weather-related careers profiled throughout this book. Their stories are a great resource for students studying careers and can be a great place to start a survey of science careers, in particular.

Directions

Divide the class into groups and assign each a weather-related career to investigate. To help get students started, you might consider reproducing the Cool Weather Career profiles on pages 10, 24, 37, 54, and 70. However, there are many more careers than the five featured here. Agricultural meteorologist, climate modeler, hurricane specialist, and tornado expert are just a few. Have students find out what the day-to-day work life is like for people in the different weather-related careers as well as what level of education is needed. Students can present their findings to the class.

Extension

Consider inviting a working meteorologist from a local TV station or nearby National Weather Service office to come speak to your class.

P O S T E R

What Causes These
Wacky Weather Events?

Inspire students to put their accumulated weather knowledge to work by showing them the eye-catching events featured on the weather phenomena poster bound in the center. Challenge student groups to find out more about these events. Students can turn their findings into informative news-story reports that feature interviews with students, neighbors, or family members who've seen such phenomena.

Book Break

Tornadoes Can Make It Rain Crabs: Weird Facts About the World's Disasters by Melvin Berger, Gilda Berger (Scholastic, 1997)

After studying about weird weather phenomena, students will enjoy reading about these weird weather facts. Invite students to use this book and the poster to create a "Weird Weather Report" they can give to the class.

Name_____

Reading a Weather Map

Forecast for Saturday

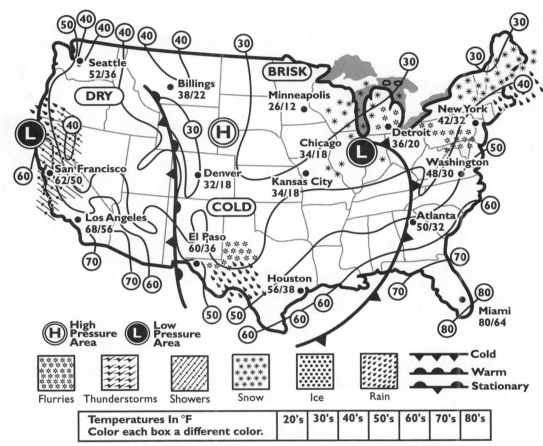

Temperatures In °F
Color each box a different color. | 20's | 30's | 40's | 50's | 60's | 70's | 80's

Questions:

1 Is the cold front on the map in the eastern or western half of the United States?
_____

2 What's the expected high temperature today in Billings, Montana?
_____

What city has that temperature for an expected low?
_____

3 What kind of front runs from Montana down through New Mexico?
_____

4 Which low-pressure area is causing snow—the one off the coast of California
or the one over Illinois?_____

5 What kind of precipitation is falling in Detroit?_____
in Vermont?_____

The Wow's and Why's of Weather Scholastic Professional Books

Mapping the Weather

Use the information below to map out a weather forecast.

The Forecast

- There will be high-pressure areas over southern California, Georgia, and the Dakotas. This will bring clear skies.

- Low-pressure areas will be over Michigan and the border between Idaho and Montana.

- An east-west stationary front is stalled running from Iowa across the middles of Illinois, Indiana, Ohio, and into Pennsylvania.

- Rain in northern Indiana and Ohio will change to snow in Michigan with flurries over northern Illinois and all of Wisconsin.

- Thunderstorms are expected in North Carolina, southern Florida, and southern Texas.

- A north-south running warm front will run along the border of Washington, Idaho, and Oregon. Showers are expected in western Washington and Oregon.

The Wow's and Why's of Weather Scholastic Professional Books

Name _____

The Weather Report

Today is _____

What's the weather like this morning/afternoon? _____

_____

_____

_____

Precipitation What kind? _____ How much? _____

Wind Direction _____ Speed _____

Air Pressure Reading _____ Rising or falling? _____

Clouds Cover: partly, half, mostly, or totally? _____

Kinds? _____

Temperature Reading _____ Hot, warm, cool, or cold? _____

Rising or falling? _____

Anything Interesting? _____

_____

_____

_____

_____

_____

_____

_____

_____

_____

Name _____

Fact or Folklore ?

Do weather sayings such as "Red sky at night, sailors' delight. Red sky at dawn, sailors be warned," hold any truth? Or are they just old sayings people used to say before barometers and thermometers were invented?

Read the six sayings below. Do you think they are true or false? Take your best guess. Then write why you think they are or aren't true.

1 Roosting birds during the day means a storm is on the way.

True   False

Why or why not? _____

_____

_____

_____

2 If a squirrel's tail is bushy in the fall, expect a hard winter.

True   False

Why or why not? _____

_____

_____

_____

3 When smoke descends, good weather ends.

True   False

Why or why not? _____

_____

_____

4 Halo 'round the moon, rain's coming soon.

True   False

Why or why not? _____

_____

_____

5 If on the 2nd of February a groundhog sees his shadow, cold winter weather will last another six weeks.

True   False

Why or why not? _____

_____

6 Moss dry, sunny sky. Moss wet, rain you'll get.

True   False

Why or why not? _____

_____

_____

_____

The Wow's and Why's of Weather Scholastic Professional Books